THE MAN OF FEELING

THE MAN
OF
FEELING

By HENRY MACKENZIE

Introduction by KENNETH C. SLAGLE
PROFESSOR OF ENGLISH, WEST CHESTER STATE COLLEGE

W · W · NORTON & COMPANY
New York · London

First published in The Norton Library
1958

W. W. Norton & Company, Inc., is the publisher of *The Norton Anthology of English Literature*, edited by M.H. Abrams *et al.*; *The Norton Anthology of Poetry*, edited by Alexander W. Allison *et al.*; *The Norton Anthology of American Literature*, edited by Nina Baym *et al.*; *The Norton Anthology of Short Fiction*, edited by R.V. Cassill; *The Norton Reader*, edited by Arthur M. Eastman *et al.*; *The Norton Anthology of Modern Poetry*, edited by Richard Ellmann and Robert O'Clair; *The Norton Anthology of Literature by Women*, edited by Sandra M. Gilbert and Susan Gubar; *The Norton Anthology of World Masterpieces*, edited by Maynard Mack *et al.*; and the Norton Critical Editions.

W. W. Norton & Company, Inc., 500 Fifth Avenue, New York, N.Y. 10110
W. W. Norton & Company Ltd., 37 Great Russell Street, London WC1B 3NU

ISBN 0-393-00214-4

INTRODUCTION
By KENNETH C. SLAGLE

An age in which one set of emotional and moral standards is normal may find strange what another time considered acceptable and even commendable. This is especially true as regards Henry Mackenzie's *The Man of Feeling*. Since its publication in 1771, literary critics have differed widely in their opinions of the book's merits. Edmund Gosse announced that Mackenzie had neither knowledge of the world nor observation of life; Henry Morley amused himself and his readers by indexing the occasions on which Mackenzie's characters shed tears. Yet J. M. S. Tompkins (*The Popular Novel in England,* p. 54), whose scholarship is probably superior to that of both earlier men, called it "the most perfect and most conscious expression after Sterne, of that type of novel which relies for interest on a delicate variety of emotional hue."

The Man of Feeling is classified as a novel of sentiment, a form which may be said to stem from Samuel Richardson. The author of *The Man of Feeling* can not hope for a place on Richardson's or Sterne's level of artistry. It was largely a combination of national pride and sympathy with his subject matter which made his fellow Scots see their "man of feeling" as the peer of Yorick, that "fellow of infinite jest." Yet Mackenzie had and has the right to a well-established position of his own.

Leading from Edinburgh Castle down through the Old Town to Holyrood House runs the Lawnmarket. Near Parliament House was Liberton's Wynd; and here Henry Mackenzie was born on August 25, 1745. His father, Dr. Joshua Mackenzie, was among the leading physicians of the city; and Henry was given the education typical of boys of his class at the High School and the University. Apparently law had a stronger attraction than medicine for Henry and he seems early to have decided on a career in the Scottish Exchequer. To prepare himself, he entered a law firm as an articled clerk. Later, when the advisability of understanding the relation of English Law to the Scottish office became clear, he went to London in 1766 for further study.

London had a strong literary fascination for Scots and it is likely that in the two years spent in the metropolis he began developing his abiding interest in letters. It seems probable that it was while living in London that he began or wrote *The Man of Feeling*. When he returned to Edinburgh in 1768, he settled in to his long and prosperous if undramatic practice of the law.

Service in the Scottish Exchequer and the office of Attorney for the Crown led him quite naturally into politics. His *Account of the Proceedings of the Parliament of 1784* brought him to the attention of William Pitt, the Younger. Their ensuing friendship probably had a great deal to do with Pitt's approval of Lord Melville's nomination of Mackenzie in 1804 to the highly desirable post of Comptroller of the Taxes for Scotland. His career was in no way unlike that of many professional men. He was a successful if not sensational lawyer, politician, husband, and parent. Parallel with these pursuits, he had another more exciting and more lasting: he was Edinburgh's "Man of Feeling."

The manuscript which he brought back from his stay in London was sent to several publishers without success. It would seem that not all of the trade agreed with Thomas Bridges' bookseller character who said "a crying volume . . . brings me more money in six months than a heavy merry thing will in six years." (*The Adventures of a Bank-Note*, p. 54.) Mackenzie was twenty-six when Cadell published *The Man of Feeling*. The book was an immediate success and gave him a literary reputation which endured, at least by courtesy, until his death in 1831.

His later novels, *The Man of the World* and *Julia de Roubigne,* are more technically skillful in plot development but less important historically. His plays and essays, although they served to aid in confirming him in his position as literary arbiter of Edinburgh, do not concern his place as a novelist. It would be negligence, on the other hand, to fail to remark on the soundness of most of his literary taste. Sir Walter Scott (who dedicated *Waverley* to him) credits Mackenzie with introducing Romantic German literature, especially the drama, to the literati of Edinburgh in a paper read to the members of the Royal Society in the spring of 1788. He was also devoted to Robert Burns and his poetry and had a part in advancing Burns' literary career.

The novel which brought Mackenzie his most lasting reputation was unusual in several particulars. With publishers striving to outdo each other in bizarre attractions, numerous experiments had been made in presenting stories to the public. Booksellers had novels on their shelves purporting to have come from manuscripts found in old desks, chests, bureaus, hackney coaches, abandoned clothes. Bilked landlords and innkeepers, guards in prisons and insane asylums, sorrowing relatives and friends had advanced "true accounts" and "real histories" by the score.

Mackenzie introduced the sporting curate with a manuscript book which had furnished frequent wadding for his fowling piece. The natural resulting mutilation served to explain a lack of connected plot and gave the author excuse for omissions and even incoherence. Even if Mackenzie had pretended an undamaged copy, there would have been small plot development. The book takes the hero to London, returns him to his home, and sees him die from an excess of sensibility.

The author did not intend that his story line should be complicated. In his subsequent novels, Mackenzie showed himself capable of technically acceptable plot construction. *The Man of Feeling,* however, was intended merely to display certain incidents which would portray the hero in a variety of emotional experiences. Each event was an opportunity to expose Harley to a relatively separate aspect of the responsiveness of sensibility. The result is an excursion through an eighteenth-century social worker's case book.

THE MAN OF FEELING

Mackenzie exercises considerable good sense and artistic skill in not having everyone whom Harley meets be a genuine object of his benevolence. The first person to appeal for alms is a "sturdy beggar" who doubles as a fortune teller. He readily admits "first I could not work, and it went against my stomach to work ever after." Mackenzie makes a rather nice distinction to explain Harley's gift to the man. "Harley had drawn a shilling from his pocket; but Virtue bade him to consider on whom he was going to bestow it. — Virtue held back his arm: — but a milder form, a younger sister of Virtue's, not so severe as Virtue nor so serious as Pity, smiled upon him: His fingers lost their compression; — nor did Virtue offer to catch the money as it fell."

His feelings are aroused by nature as well as man. This interest in landscape as a setting and for itself is less common in the novel of sentiment than in other types. Mackenzie's work in this particular displays an interesting relationship with the Gothic novel in his use of the picturesque. There are earlier touches of his connoisseurship of the scenic; but his description of the old soldier lying asleep under a tree is deliberately and admittedly reminiscent of Salvator Rosa. This artist, so frequently mentioned in Ann Radcliffe and her group, is new to the novel of sentiment.

Harley's death is in keeping with the spirit of the man and the expressed intention of the book. Hearing that Miss Walton is about to marry Sir Harry Benson, the man of feeling is heartbroken in spite of his never having been able to tell her of his love. Even when he discovers that the report is false, his modesty and reticence bar his speaking. Only when he is in a final decline, brought on directly by his nursing of Old Edwards but indirectly by his weariness of the world's pain, does he speak. Miss Walton answers in a rather charming speech of mixed reserve and sensibility:

— "Let me intreat you," said she, "to have better hopes — Let not life be so indifferent to you; if my wishes can put any value on it — I will not pretend to misunderstand you—I know your worth—I have known it long

THE MAN OF FEELING

— I have esteemed it — What would you have me say!
— I have loved it as it deserved."

The shock of joy was too much. After taking her hand Harley falls dead and Miss Walton swoons in grief.

But the novel offers far more than fustian passages of sighs and tears. Harley is no milk-lipped boy for all his sensitivity. He silences the officer in the stage coach and courageously faces Atkins' sword. Nor is he impractical in meeting the problems of other people; only his own defeat him.

For all the book's real or assumed humility, there are pointed touches of satire. The stage-coach passage shows him in the satirical tradition of Addison and Steele. With the swindlers and the press gang Mackenzie follows Richardson by introducing rough realisms to emphasize the sentiment to follow. The author understood clearly that the man of feeling did not live in a world of feeling, but in a world in which only occasionally were indifference and inhumanity overcome by the dictates of sensibility.

To what extent Sterne influenced the book is hard to evaluate. Mackenzie denied having read the *Sentimental Journey* and even insisted, "certain it is that some parts of *The Man of Feeling* which bear the strongest resemblance to the *Sentimental Journey* were written, and even read to some of my friends before the publication of that ingenious performance." In spite of this denial, genuine as it seems and honorable as is the man who made it, it seems strange that the young Scot was not at least indirectly influenced by Sterne. Perhaps Harry Brooke's *The Fool of Quality* may have been more influential. Brooke's hero wanders from one adventure in responsiveness to another until the reader is stunned by his benevolence and suffocated by his sentimentality. Mackenzie is much less prodigal in both aspects. His use of sensibility is at once more genuine than the pawky exploitation of Sterne, more believable than the prodigal largess of tens of thousands of pounds in a season by Brooke. Sir Walter Scott's observation that Harley is "a hero constantly obedient to every emotion of his moral sense" is of key importance in understanding Mackenzie.

THE MAN OF FEELING

It must be remembered that responsiveness to sensibility was considered to indicate the truly perceptive mind. Harley was even in his own day recognized as a paragon. If he were elevated above the average man's achievement, he was not beyond understanding and emulation. Civilization had been long in developing the man of feeling; and to be considered one, the individual had constantly to test his own responsiveness lest he become hardened by life's daily, practical contacts.

The world was learning humanity. In this respect the novel of sentiment is closely related to the social consciousness inherent in the romantic movement. The eighteenth-century men and women who literally wept over the world's distresses began fumblingly to try to alleviate them. The Victorians, only a little less obviously sentimental, organized charitable societies. Today, aid to the underprivileged is international in scope; but among its progenitors is Harley, who gave tears and alms to the distressed.

THE MAN OF FEELING

INTRODUCTION

MY dog had made a point on a piece of fallow-ground, and led the curate and me two or three hundred yards over that and some stubble adjoining, in a breathless state of expectation, on a burning first of September.

It was a false point, and our labour was vain: yet, to do Rover justice (for he's an excellent dog, though I have lost his pedigree), the fault was none of his, the birds were gone: the curate showed me the spot where they had lain basking, at the root of an old hedge.

I stopped and cried Hem! The curate is fatter than I; he wiped the sweat from his brow.

There is no state where one is apter to pause and look round one, than after such a disappointment. It is even so in life. When we have been hurrying on, impelled by some warm wish or other, looking neither to the right hand nor to the left—we find of a sudden that all our gay hopes are flown; and the only slender consolation that some friend can give us, is to point where they were once to be found. And if we are not of that combustible race, who will rather beat their heads in spite, than wipe their brows with the curate, we look round and say, with the nauseated listlessness of the king of Israel, " All is vanity and vexation of spirit."

I looked round with some such grave apophthegm in my mind when I discovered, for the first time, a venerable pile, to which the enclosure belonged. An air of melancholy hung about it. There was a languid stillness in the day, and a single crow, that perched on an old tree by the side of the gate, seemed to delight in the echo of its own croaking.

I leaned on my gun and looked; but I had not breath

enough to ask the curate a question. I observed carving on the bark of some of the trees: 'twas indeed the only mark of human art about the place, except that some branches appeared to have been lopped, to give a view of the cascade, which was formed by a little rill at some distance.

Just at that instant I saw pass between the trees a young lady with a book in her hand. I stood upon a stone to observe her; but the curate sat him down on the grass, and leaning his back where I stood, told me, "That was the daughter of a neighbouring gentleman of the name of WALTON, whom he had seen walking there more than once.

"Some time ago," he said, "one HARLEY lived there, a whimsical sort of a man I am told, but I was not then in the cure; though, if I had a turn for such things, I might know a good deal of his history, for the greatest part of it is still in my possession."

"His history!" said I. "Nay, you may call it what you please," said the curate; "for indeed it is no more a history than it is a sermon. The way I came by it was this: some time ago, a grave, oddish kind of a man boarded at a farmer's in this parish: the country people called him The Ghost; and he was known by the slouch in his gait, and the length of his stride. I was but little acquainted with him, for he never frequented any of the clubs hereabouts. Yet for all he used to walk a-nights, he was as gentle as a lamb at times; for I have seen him playing at teetotum with the children, on the great stone at the door of our churchyard.

"Soon after I was made curate, he left the parish, and went nobody knows whither; and in his room was found a bundle of papers, which was brought to me by his landlord. I began to read them, but I soon grew weary of the task; for, besides that the hand is intolerably bad, I could never find the author in one strain for two chapters together; and I don't believe there's a single syllogism from beginning to end."

INTRODUCTION

" I should be glad to see this medley," said I. " You shall see it now," answered the curate, " for I always take it along with me a-shooting." " How came it so torn?" " 'Tis excellent wadding," said the curate.—This was a plea of expediency I was not in a condition to answer; for I had actually in my pocket great part of an edition of one of the German Illustrissimi, for the very same purpose. We exchanged books; and by that means (for the curate is a strenuous logician) we probably saved both.

When I returned to town, I had leisure to peruse the acquisition I had made: I found it a bundle of little episodes, put together without art, and of no importance on the whole, with something of nature, and little else in them. I was a good deal affected with some very trifling passages in it; and had the name of Marmontel, or a Richardson, been on the title-page——'tis odds that I should have wept: But

One is ashamed to be pleased with the works of one knows not whom.

CHAPTER XI[1]

OF BASHFULNESS—A CHARACTER—HIS OPINION ON
THAT SUBJECT

THERE is some rust about every man at the beginning;
though in some nations (among the French for instance) the ideas of the inhabitants, from climate, or what
other cause you will, are so vivacious, so eternally on the wing,
that they must, even in small societies, have a frequent colli-
sion; the rust therefore will wear off sooner: but in Britain
it often goes with a man to his grave, nay, he dares not even
pen a *hic jacet* to speak out for him after his death.

"Let them rub it off by travel," said the baronet's brother,
who was a striking instance of excellent metal, shamefully
rusted. I had drawn my chair near his. Let me paint the
honest old man: 'tis but one passing sentence to preserve his
image in my mind.

He sat in his usual attitude, with his elbow rested on his
knee, and his fingers pressed to his cheek. His face was
shaded by his hand; yet it was a face that might once have
been well accounted handsome; its features were manly and
striking, and a certain dignity resided on his eye-brows, which
were the largest I remember to have seen. His person was
tall and well-made; but the indolence of his nature had now
inclined it to corpulency.

His remarks were few, and made only to his familiar
friends; but they were such as the world might have heard

[1] The reader will remember that the Editor is accountable only for
scattered chapters and fragments of chapters; the curate must answer
for the rest. The number at the top, when the chapter was entire, he
has given as it originally stood, with the title which its author had
affixed to it.

with veneration: and his heart, uncorrupted by its ways, was ever warm in the cause of virtue and his friends.

He is now forgotten and gone! The last time I was at Silton Hall, I saw his chair stand in its corner by the fire-side; there was an additional cushion on it, and it was occupied by my young lady's favourite lap-dog. I drew near unperceived, and pinched its ears in the bitterness of my soul; the creature howled, and ran to its mistress. She did not suspect the author of its misfortune, but she bewailed it in the most pathetic terms; and kissing its lips, laid it gently on her lap, and covered it with a cambric handkerchief. I sat in my old friend's seat; I heard the roar of mirth and gaiety around me: poor Ben Silton! I gave thee a tear then: accept of one cordial drop that falls to thy memory now.

"Let them rub it off by travel."—Why, it is true, said I, that will go far; but then it will often happen, that in the velocity of a modern tour, and amidst the materials through which it is commonly made, the friction is so violent, that not only the rust, but the metal too, will be lost in the progress.

"Give me leave to correct the expression of your metaphor," said Mr. Silton, " this covering of which you complain, is not always rust which is produced by the inactivity of the body on which it preys; such, perhaps, is the case with me, though indeed I was never cleared from my youth; but (taking it in its first stage) it is rather an encrustation, which nature has given for purposes of the greatest wisdom."

"You are right," I returned; " and sometimes, like certain precious fossils, there may be hid under it gems of the purest brilliancy."

"Nay, farther," continued Mr. Silton, " there are two distinct sorts of what we call bashfulness; this, the awkwardness of a booby, which a few steps into the world will convert into the pertness of a coxcomb; that, a consciousness, which the most delicate feelings produce, and the most extensive knowledge cannot always remove."

From the incidents I have already related, I imagine it will be concluded that Harley was of the latter species of bashful animals; at least, if Mr. Silton's principle be just, it may be argued on this side; for the gradation of the first mentioned sort, it is certain, he never attained. Some part of his external

appearance was modelled from the company of those gentlemen, whom the antiquity of a family, now possessed of bare
£250 a year, entitled its representative to approach: these indeed were not many; great part of the property in his neighbourhood being in the hands of merchants, who had got rich
by their lawful calling abroad, and the sons of stewards, who
had got rich by their lawful calling at home: persons so perfectly versed in the ceremonial of thousands, tens of thousands, and hundreds of thousands (whose degrees of precedency are plainly demonstrable from the first page of the
Complete Accomptant, or Young Man's Best Pocket Companion) that a bow at church from them to such a man as
Harley would have made the parson look back into his sermon
for some precept of Christian humility.

CHAPTER XII

OF WORLDLY INTERESTS

THERE are certain interests which the world supposes
every man to have, and which therefore are properly
enough termed worldly; but the world is apt to make an er-
roneous estimate: ignorant of the dispositions which consti-
tute our happiness or misery, it brings to an undistinguished
scale the means of the one, as connected with power, wealth,
or grandeur, and of the other with their contraries. Philosophers and poets have often protested against this decision;
but their arguments have been despised as declamatory, or
ridiculed as romantic.

There are never wanting to a young man some grave and
prudent friends to set him right in this particular, if he need
it; to watch his ideas as they arise, and point them to those
objects which a wise man should never forget.

Harley did not want for some monitors of this sort. He
was frequently told of men whose fortunes enabled them to
command all the luxuries of life, whose fortunes were of their
own acquirement: his envy was excited by a description of
their happiness, and his emulation by a recital of the means
which had procured it.

THE MAN OF FEELING

Harley was apt to hear those lectures with indifference; nay, sometimes they got the better of his temper; and as the instances were not always amiable, provoked, on his part, some reflections, which I am persuaded his good-nature would else have avoided.

Indeed, I have observed one ingredient, somewhat necessary in a man's composition towards happiness, which people of feeling would do well to acquire; a certain respect for the follies of mankind: for there are so many fools whom the opinion of the world entitles to regard, whom accident has placed in heights of which they are unworthy, that he who cannot restrain his contempt or indignation at the sight will be too often quarrelling with the disposal of things to relish that share which is allotted to himself. I do not mean, however, to insinuate this to have been the case with Harley; on the contrary, if we might rely on his own testimony, the conceptions he had of pomp and grandeur served to endear the state which Providence had assigned him.

He lost his father, the last surviving of his parents, as I have already related, when he was a boy. The good man, from a fear of offending, as well as from a regard to his son, had named him a variety of guardians; one consequence of which was, that they seldom met at all to consider the affairs of their ward; and when they did meet, their opinions were so opposite, that the only possible method of conciliation was the mediatory power of a dinner and a bottle, which commonly interrupted, not ended, the dispute; and after that interruption ceased, left the consulting parties in a condition not very proper for adjusting it. His education therefore had been but indifferently attended to; and after being taken from a country school, at which he had been boarded, the young gentleman was suffered to be his own master in the subsequent branches of literature, with some assistance from the parson of the parish in languages and philosophy, and from the exciseman in arithmetic and bookkeeping. One of his guardians, indeed, who, in his youth, had been an inhabitant of the Temple, set him to read Coke upon Lyttelton: a book which is very properly put into the hands of beginners in that science, as its simplicity is accommodated to their understandings, and its size to their inclination. He profited but little by the perusal; but it was not without its use in the family: for his maiden aunt applied it commonly to the laudable purpose of pressing her rebellious linens to the folds she had allotted them.

There were particularly two ways of increasing his fortune, which might have occurred to people of less foresight than the counsellors we have mentioned. One of these was, the prospect of his succeeding to an old lady, a distant relation, who was known to be possessed of a very large sum in the stocks: but in this their hopes were disappointed; for the young man was so untoward in his disposition, that, notwithstanding the instructions he daily received, his visits rather tended to alienate than gain the good-will of his kinswoman. He sometimes looked grave when the old lady told the jokes of her youth; he often refused to eat when she pressed him, and was seldom or never provided with sugar-candy or liquorice when she was seized with a fit of coughing: nay, he had once the rudeness to fall asleep while she was describing the composition and virtues of her favourite cholic-water. In short, he accommodated himself so ill to her humour, that she died, and did not leave him a farthing.

The other method pointed out to him was an endeavour to get a lease of some crown-lands, which lay contiguous to his little paternal estate. This, it was imagined, might be easily procured, as the crown did not draw so much rent as Harley could afford to give, with very considerable profit to himself; and the then lessee had rendered himself so obnoxious to the ministry, by the disposal of his vote at an election, that he could not expect a renewal. This, however, needed some interest with the great, which Harley or his father never possessed.

His neighbour, Mr. Walton, having heard of this affair, generously offered his assistance to accomplish it. He told him, that though he had long been a stranger to courtiers, yet he believed there were some of them who might pay regard to his recommendation; and that, if he thought it worth the while to take a London journey upon the business, he would furnish him with a letter of introduction to a baronet of his acquaintance, who had a great deal to say with the first lord of the treasury.

When his friends heard of this offer, they pressed him with the utmost earnestness to accept of it. They did not fail to enumerate the many advantages which a certain degree of spirit and assurance gives a man who would make a figure in the world: they repeated their instances of good fortune in others, ascribed them all to a happy forwardness of disposition; and made so copious a recital of the disadvantages which attend the opposite weakness, that a stranger, who had heard them, would have been led to imagine, that in the British code there was some disqualifying statute against any citizen who should be convicted of—modesty.

Harley, though he had no great relish for the attempt, yet could not resist the torrent of motives that assaulted him; and as he needed but little preparation for his journey, a day, not very distant, was fixed for his departure.

———

CHAPTER XIII

THE MAN OF FEELING IN LOVE

THE day before that on which he set out, he went to take leave of Mr. Walton.—We would conceal nothing;—there was another person of the family to whom also the visit was intended, on whose account, perhaps, there were some tenderer feelings in the bosom of Harley than his gratitude for the friendly notice of that gentleman (though he was seldom deficient in that virtue) could inspire. Mr. Walton had a daughter; and such a daughter! we will attempt some description of her by and by.

Harley's notions of the καλον, or beautiful, were not always to be defined, nor indeed such as the world would always assent to, though we could define them. A blush, a phrase of affability to an inferior, a tear at a moving tale, were to him, like the Cestus of Cytherea, unequalled in conferring beauty. For all these Miss Walton was remarkable; but as these, like the above-mentioned Cestus, are perhaps still more powerful when the wearer is possessed of some degree of beauty, commonly so called, it happened, that, from this cause, they had more than usual power in the person of that young lady.

She was now arrived at that period of life which takes, or is supposed to take, from the flippancy of girlhood those sprightlinesses with which some good-natured old maids oblige the world at three-score. She had been ushered into life (as that word is used in the dialect of St. James's) at seventeen, her father being then in parliament, and living in London: at seventeen, therefore, she had been a universal toast; her health, now she was four-and-twenty, was only drank by those who knew her face at least. Her complexion was mellowed into a paleness, which certainly took from her beauty; but agreed, at least Harley used to say so, with the pensive softness of her mind. Her eyes were of that gentle hazel colour which is rather mild than piercing; and, except when they were lighted up by good-humour, which was frequently the case, were supposed by the fine gentlemen to want fire. Her air and manner were elegant in the highest degree, and were as sure of commanding respect as their mistress was far from demanding it. Her voice was inexpressibly soft; it was, according to that incomparable simile of Otway's,

> ————"like the shepherd's pipe upon the mountains,
> When all his little flock's at feed before him."

The effect it had upon Harley, himself used to paint ridiculously enough; and ascribed it to powers, which few believed, and nobody cared for.

Her conversation was always cheerful, but rarely witty; and without the smallest affectation of learning, had as much sentiment in it as would have puzzled a Turk, upon his principles of female materialism, to account for. Her beneficence was unbounded; indeed the natural tenderness of her heart might have been argued, by the frigidity of a casuist, as detracting from her virtue in this respect, for her humanity was a feeling, not a principle: but minds like Harley's are not very apt to make this distinction, and generally give our virtue credit for all that benevolence which is instinctive in our nature.

As her father had for some years retired to the country, Harley had frequent opportunities of seeing her. He looked on her for some time merely with that respect and admiration which her appearance seemed to demand, and the opinion of others conferred upon her: from this cause, perhaps, and from that extreme sensibility of which we have taken frequent notice, Harley was remarkably silent in her presence. He heard her sentiments with peculiar attention, sometimes with looks very expressive of approbation; but seldom declared his opinion on the subject, much less made compliments to the lady on the justness of her remarks.

From this very reason it was that Miss Walton frequently took more particular notice of him than of other visitors, who, by the laws of precedency, were better entitled to it: it was a mode of politeness she had peculiarly studied, to bring to the line of that equality, which is ever necessary for the ease of our guests, those whose sensibility had placed them below it.

Harley saw this; for though he was a child in the drama of the world, yet was it not altogether owing to a want of knowledge of his part; on the contrary, the most delicate consciousness of propriety often kindled that blush which marred the performance of it: this raised his esteem something above what the most sanguine descriptions of her goodness had been able to do; for certain it is, that notwithstanding the laboured definitions which very wise men have given us of the inherent beauty of virtue, we are always inclined to think her handsomest when she condescends to smile upon ourselves.

It would be trite to observe the easy gradation from esteem to love: in the bosom of Harley there scarce needed a transition; for there were certain seasons when his ideas were flushed to a degree much above their common complexion. In times not credulous of inspiration, we should account for this from some natural cause; but we do not mean to account for it at all; it were sufficient to describe its effects; but they were sometimes so ludicrous, as might derogate from the dignity of the sensations which produced them to describe. They were treated indeed as such by most of Harley's sober friends, who often laughed very heartily at the awkward blunders of the real Harley, when the different faculties, which should have prevented them, were entirely occupied by the ideal. In some of these paroxysms of fancy, Miss Walton did not fail to be introduced; and the picture which had been drawn amidst the surrounding objects of unnoticed levity was now singled out to be viewed through the medium of romantic imagination: it was improved of course, and esteem was a word inexpressive of the feelings which it excited.

CHAPTER XIV

HE SETS OUT ON HIS JOURNEY—THE BEGGAR AND HIS DOG

H E had taken leave of his aunt on the eve of his intended departure; but the good lady's affection for her nephew interrupted her sleep, and early as it was next morning when Harley came downstairs to set out, he found her in the parlour with a tear on her cheek, and her caudle-cup in her hand. She knew enough of physic to prescribe against going abroad of a morning with an empty stomach. She gave her blessing with the draught; her instructions she had delivered the night before. They consisted mostly of negatives, for London, in her idea, was so replete with temptations that it needed the whole armour of her friendly cautions to repel their attacks.

Peter stood at the door. We have mentioned this faithful fellow formerly: Harley's father had taken him up an orphan, and saved him from being cast on the parish; and he had ever since remained in the service of him and of his son. Harley shook him by the hand as he passed, smiling, as if he had said, " I will not weep." He sprung hastily into the chaise that waited for him; Peter folded up the step. " My dear master," said he, shaking the solitary lock that hung on either side of his head, " I have been told as how London is a sad place." He was choked with the thought, and his benediction could not be heard:—but it shall be heard, honest Peter! where these tears will add to its energy.

In a few hours Harley reached the inn where he proposed breakfasting, but the fulness of his heart would not suffer him to eat a morsel. He walked out on the road, and gaining a little height, stood gazing on the quarter he had left. He looked for his wonted prospect, his fields, his woods, and his hills: they were lost in the distant clouds! He pencilled them on the clouds, and bade them farewell with a sigh!

He sat down on a large stone to take out a little pebble from his shoe, when he saw, at some distance, a beggar approaching him. He had on a loose sort of coat, mended with different-coloured rags, amongst which the blue and the russet were the predominant. He had a short knotty stick in his hand, and on the top of it was stuck a ram's horn; his knees (though he was no pilgrim) had worn the stuff of his breeches; he wore no shoes, and his stockings had entirely lost that part of them which should have covered his feet and ankles; in his face, however, was the plump appearance of good humour; he walked a good round pace, and a crook-legged dog trotted at his heels.

"Our delicacies," said Harley to himself, "are fantastic; they are not in nature! that beggar walks over the sharpest of these stones barefooted, whilst I have lost the most delightful dream in the world, from the smallest of them happening to get into my shoe." The beggar had by this time come up, and, pulling off a piece of hat, asked charity of Harley; the dog began to beg too:—it was impossible to resist both; and, in truth, the want of shoes and stockings had made both unnecessary, for Harley had destined sixpence for him before. The beggar, on receiving it, poured forth blessings without number; and, with a sort of smile on his countenance, said to Harley "that if he wanted to have his fortune told"—Harley turned his eye briskly on the beggar: it was an unpromising look for the subject of a prediction, and silenced the prophet immediately. "I would much rather learn," said Harley, "what it is in your power to tell me: your trade must be an entertaining one; sit down on this stone, and let me know something of your profession; I have often thought of turning fortune-teller for a week or two myself."

"Master," replied the beggar, "I like your frankness much; God knows I had the humour of plain-dealing in me from a child, but there is no doing with it in this world; we must live as we can, and lying is, as you call it, my profession, but I was in some sort forced to the trade, for I dealt once in telling truth.

"I was a labourer, sir, and gained as much as to make me live: I never laid by indeed: for I was reckoned a piece of a wag, and your wags, I take it, are seldom rich, Mr. Harley."

12

THE MAN OF FEELING

"So," said Harley, "you seem to know me."

"Ay, there are few folks in the country that I don't know something of: how should I tell fortunes else?"

"True; but to go on with your story: you were a labourer, you say, and a wag; your industry, I suppose, you left with your old trade, but your humour you preserve to be of use to you in your new."

"What signifies sadness, sir? a man grows lean on't: but I was brought to my idleness by degrees; first I could not work, and it went against my stomach to work ever after. I was seized with a jail fever at the time of the assizes being in the county where I lived; for I was always curious to get acquainted with the felons, because they are commonly fellows of much mirth and little thought, qualities I had ever an esteem for. In the height of this fever, Mr. Harley, the house where I lay took fire, and burnt to the ground; I was carried out in that condition, and lay all the rest of my illness in a barn. I got the better of my disease, however, but I was so weak that I spit blood whenever I attempted to work. I had no relation living that I knew of, and I never kept a friend above a week, when I was able to joke; I seldom remained above six months in a parish, so that I might have died before I had found a settlement in any: thus I was forced to beg my bread, and a sorry trade I found it, Mr. Harley. I told all my misfortunes truly, but they were seldom believed; and the few who gave me a halfpenny as they passed did it with a shake of the head, and an injunction not to trouble them with a long story. In short, I found that people don't care to give alms without some security for their money; a wooden leg or a withered arm is a sort of draught upon heaven for those who choose to have their money placed to account there; so I changed my plan, and, instead of telling my own misfortunes, began to prophesy happiness to others. This I found by much the better way: folks will always listen when the tale is their own, and of many who say they do not believe in fortune-telling, I have known few on whom it had not a very sensible effect. I pick up the names of their acquaintance; amours and little squabbles are easily gleaned among servants and neighbours; and indeed people themselves are the best

13

intelligencers in the world for our purpose: they dare not puzzle us for their own sakes, for every one is anxious to hear what they wish to believe, and they who repeat it, to laugh at it when they have done, are generally more serious than their hearers are apt to imagine. With a tolerable good memory, and some share of cunning, with the help of walking a-nights over heaths and church-yards, with this, and showing the tricks of that there dog, whom I stole from the serjeant of a marching regiment (and by the way, he can steal too upon occasion), I make shift to pick up a livelihood. My trade, indeed, is none of the honestest; yet people are not much cheated neither who give a few halfpence for a prospect of happiness, which I have heard some persons say is all a man can arrive at in this world. But I must bid you good day, sir, for I have three miles to walk before noon, to inform some boarding-school young ladies whether their husbands are to be peers of the realm or captains in the army: a question which I promised to answer them by that time."

Harley had drawn a shilling from his pocket; but Virtue bade him consider on whom he was going to bestow it. Virtue held back his arm; but a milder form, a younger sister of Virtue's, not so severe as Virtue, nor so serious as Pity, smiled upon him; his fingers lost their compression, nor did Virtue offer to catch the money as it fell. It had no sooner reached the ground than the watchful cur (a trick he had been taught) snapped it up, and, contrary to the most approved method of stewardship, delivered it immediately into the hands of his master.

———

CHAPTER XIX

HE MAKES A SECOND EXPEDITION TO THE BARONET'S—THE
LAUDABLE AMBITION OF A YOUNG MAN TO BE THOUGHT
SOMETHING BY THE WORLD

WE have related, in a former chapter, the little success of his first visit to the great man, for whom he had the introductory letter from Mr. Walton. To people of equal sensibility, the influence of those trifles we mentioned on his deportment will not appear surprising, but to his friends in the country they could not be stated, nor would they have allowed them any place in the account. In some of their letters, therefore, which he received soon after, they expressed their surprise at his not having been more urgent in his application, and again recommended the blushless assiduity of successful merit.

He resolved to make another attempt at the baronet's; fortified with higher notions of his own dignity, and with less apprehension of repulse. In his way to Grosvenor Square he began to ruminate on the folly of mankind, who affixed those ideas of superiority to riches, which reduced the minds of men, by nature equal with the more fortunate, to that sort of servility which he felt in his own. By the time he had reached the Square, and was walking along the pavement which led to the baronet's, he had brought his reasoning on the subject to such a point, that the conclusion, by every rule of logic, should have led him to a thorough indifference in his approaches to a fellow-mortal, whether that fellow-mortal was possessed of six or six thousand pounds a year. It is probable, however, that the premises had been improperly formed: for it is certain, that when he approached the great man's door he felt his heart agitated by an unusual pulsation.

He had almost reached it, when he observed a young gentleman coming out, dressed in a white frock and a red laced waistcoat, with a small switch in his hand, which he seemed to manage with a particular good grace. As he passed him on the steps, the stranger very politely made him a bow, which Harley returned, though he could not remember ever having seen him before. He asked Harley, in the same civil manner, if he was going to wait on his friend the baronet. " For I was just calling," said he, " and am sorry to find that he is gone for some days into the country."

Harley thanked him for his information, and was turning from the door, when the other observed that it would be proper to leave his name, and very obligingly knocked for that purpose.

" Here is a gentleman, Tom, who meant to have waited on your master."

" Your name, if you please, sir ? "

" Harley."

"You'll remember, Tom, Harley."

The door was shut. "Since we are here," said he, "we shall not lose our walk if we add a little to it by a turn or two in Hyde Park."

He accompanied this proposal with a second bow, and Harley accepted of it by another in return.

The conversation, as they walked, was brilliant on the side of his companion. The playhouse, the opera, with every occurrence in high life, he seemed perfectly master of, and talked of some reigning beauties of quality in a manner the most feeling in the world. Harley admired the happiness of his vivacity, and, opposite as it was to the reserve of his own nature, began to be much pleased with its effects.

Though I am not of opinion with some wise men, that the existence of objects depends on idea, yet I am convinced that their appearance is not a little influenced by it. The optics of some minds are so unhappily constructed as to throw a certain shade on every picture that is presented to them, while those of others (of which number was Harley), like the mirrors of the ladies, have a wonderful effect in bettering their complexions. Through such a medium perhaps he was looking on his present companion.

When they had finished their walk, and were returning by the corner of the Park, they observed a board hung out of a window signifying, "An excellent ORDINARY on Saturdays and Sundays." It happened to be Saturday, and the table was covered.

"What if we should go in and dine here, if you happen not to be engaged, sir?" said the young gentleman. "It is not impossible but we shall meet with some original or other; it is a sort of humour I like hugely."

Harley made no objection, and the stranger showed him the way into the parlour.

He was placed, by the courtesy of his introductor, in an arm-chair that stood at one side of the fire. Over against him was seated a man of a grave considering aspect, with that look of sober prudence which indicates what is commonly called a warm man. He wore a pretty large wig, which had once been white, but was now of a brownish yellow; his coat was one of those modest-coloured drabs which mock the injuries of dust and dirt; two jack-boots concealed, in part, the well-mended knees of an old pair of buckskin breeches; while the spotted handkerchief round his neck preserved at once its owner from catching cold and his neckcloth from being dirtied. Next him sat another man, with a tankard in his hand and a quid of tobacco in his cheek, whose eye was rather more vivacious, and whose dress was something smarter.

The first-mentioned gentleman took notice that the room had been so lately washed, as not to have had time to dry, and remarked that wet lodging was unwholesome for man or beast. He looked round at the same time for a poker to stir the fire with, which, he at last observed to the company, the people of the house had removed in order to save their coals. This difficulty, however, he overcame by the help of Harley's stick, saying, " that as they should, no doubt, pay for their fire in some shape or other, he saw no reason why they should not have the use of it while they sat."

The door was now opened for the admission of dinner. " I don't know how it is with you, gentlemen," said Harley's new acquaintance, " but I am afraid I shall not be able to get down a morsel at this horrid mechanical hour of dining." He sat down, however, and did not show any want of appetite by his eating. He took upon him the carving of the meat, and criticised on the goodness of the pudding.

When the table-cloth was removed, he proposed calling for some punch, which was readily agreed to; he seemed at first inclined to make it himself, but afterwards changed his mind, and left that province to the waiter, telling him to have it pure West Indian, or he could not taste a drop of it.

When the punch was brought he undertook to fill the glasses and call the toasts. " The King."—The toast naturally produced politics. It is the privilege of Englishmen to drink the king's health, and to talk of his conduct. The man who sat opposite to Harley (and who by this time, partly from himself, and partly from his acquaintance on his left hand, was discovered to be a grazier) observed, " That it was a shame for so many pensioners to be allowed to take the bread out of the mouth of the poor."

" Ay, and provisions," said his friend, " were never so dear in the memory of man; I wish the king and his counsellors would look to that."

"As for the matter of provisions, neighbour Wrightson," he replied, "I am sure the prices of cattle——"

A dispute would have probably ensued, but it was prevented by the spruce toastmaster, who gave a sentiment, and turning to the two politicians, "Pray, gentlemen," said he, "let us have done with these musty politics: I would always leave them to the beer-suckers in Butcher Row.[1] Come, let us have something of the fine arts. That was a damn'd hard match between the Nailor and Tim Bucket. The knowing ones were cursedly taken in there! I lost a cool hundred myself, faith."

At mention of the cool hundred, the grazier threw his eyes aslant, with a mingled look of doubt and surprise; while the man at his elbow looked arch, and gave a short emphatical sort of cough.

Both seemed to be silenced, however, by this intelligence; and while the remainder of the punch lasted the conversation was wholly engrossed by the gentleman with the fine waistcoat, who told a great many "immense comical stories" and "confounded smart things," as he termed them, acted and spoken by lords, ladies, and young bucks of quality, of his acquaintance. At last, the grazier, pulling out a watch, of a very unusual size, and telling the hour, said that he had an appointment. "Is it so late?" said the young gentleman; "then I am afraid I have missed an appointment already; but the truth is, I am cursedly given to missing of appointments."

When the grazier and he were gone, Harley turned to the remaining personage, and asked him if he knew that young gentleman. "A gentleman!" said he; "ay, he is one of your gentlemen at the top of an affidavit. I knew him, some years ago, in the quality of a footman; and I believe he had some times the honour to be a pimp. At last, some of the great folks, to whom he had been serviceable in both capacities, had him made a gauger; in which station he remains, and has the assurance to pretend an acquaintance with men of quality.

[1] It may be necessary to inform readers of the present day, that the noted political debating Society, called the *Robinhood*, was held in a house in Butcher Row.

The impudent dog! with a few shillings in his pocket, he will talk you three times as much as my friend Mundy there, who is worth nine thousand if he's worth a farthing, But I know the rascal, and despise him, as he deserves."

Harley began to despise him too, and to conceive some indignation at having sat with patience to hear such a fellow speak nonsense. But he corrected himself by reflecting that he was perhaps as well entertained, and instructed too, by this same modest gauger, as he should have been by such a man as he had thought proper to personate. And surely the fault may more properly be imputed to that rank where the futility is real than where it is feigned: to that rank whose opportunities for nobler accomplishments have only served to rear a fabric of folly which the untutored hand of affectation, even among the meanest of mankind, can imitate with success.

———

CHAPTER XX

HE VISITS BEDLAM—THE DISTRESSES OF A DAUGHTER

OF those things called Sights in London, which every stranger is supposed desirous to see, Bedlam is one. To that place, therefore, an acquaintance of Harley's, after having accompanied him to several other shows, proposed a visit. Harley objected to it, " because," said he, " I think it an inhuman practice to expose the greatest misery with which our nature is afflicted to every idle visitant who can afford a trifling perquisite to the keeper; especially as it is a distress which the humane must see, with the painful reflection, that it is not in their power to alleviate it." He was overpowered, however, by the solicitations of his friend and the other persons of the party (amongst whom were several ladies); and they went in a body to Moorfields.

Their conductor led them first to the dismal mansions of those who are in the most horrid state of incurable madness. The clanking of chains, the wildness of their cries, and the imprecations which some of them uttered, formed a scene inexpressibly shocking. Harley and his companions, especially the female part of them, begged their guide to return; he seemed surprised at their uneasiness, and was with difficulty prevailed on to leave that part of the house without showing them some others: who, as he expressed it in the phrase of those that keep wild beasts for show, were much better worth seeing than any they had passed, being ten times more fierce and unmanageable.

He led them next to that quarter where those reside who, as they are not dangerous to themselves or others, enjoy a certain degree of freedom, according to the state of their distemper.

Harley had fallen behind his companions, looking at a man who was making pendulums with bits of thread and little balls of clay. He had delineated a segment of a circle on the wall with chalk, and marked their different vibrations by intersecting it with cross lines. A decent-looking man came up, and smiling at the maniac, turned to Harley, and told him that gentleman had once been a very celebrated mathematician. "He fell a sacrifice," said he, "to the theory of comets; for having, with infinite labour, formed a table on the conjectures of Sir Isaac Newton, he was disappointed in the return of one of those luminaries, and was very soon after obliged to be placed here by his friends. If you please to follow me, sir," continued the stranger, "I believe I shall be able to give a more satisfactory account of the unfortunate people you see here than the man who attends your companions." Harley bowed, and accepted his offer.

The next person they came up to had scrawled a variety of figures on a piece of slate. Harley had the curiosity to take a nearer view of them. They consisted of different columns, on the top of which were marked South-sea annuities, India-stock, and Three per cent. annuities consol. "This," said Harley's instructor, "was a gentleman well known in Change Alley. He was once worth fifty thousand pounds, and had actually agreed for the purchase of an estate in the West, in order to realise his money; but he quarrelled with the proprietor about the repairs of the garden wall, and so returned to town, to follow his old trade of stock-jobbing a little longer; when an unlucky fluctuation of stock, in which he was engaged to an immense extent, reduced him at once to poverty and to madness. Poor wretch! he told me t'other day that against the next payment of differences he should be some hundreds above a plum."

"It is a spondee, and I will maintain it," interrupted a voice on his left hand. This assertion was followed by a very rapid recital of some verses from Homer. "That figure," said the gentleman, "whose clothes are so bedaubed with snuff, was a schoolmaster of some reputation: he came hither to be resolved of some doubts he entertained concerning the genuine pronunciation of the Greek vowels. In his highest fits, he makes frequent mention of one Mr. Bentley.

"But delusive ideas, sir, are the motives of the greatest part of mankind, and a heated imagination the power by which their actions are incited: the world, in the eye of a philosopher, may be said to be a large madhouse." "It is true," answered Harley, "the passions of men are temporary madnesses; and sometimes very fatal in their effects.

From Macedonia's madman to the Swede."

"It was, indeed," said the stranger, "a very mad thing in Charles to think of adding so vast a country as Russia to his dominions: that would have been fatal indeed; the balance of the North would then have been lost; but the Sultan and I would never have allowed it."——"Sir!" said Harley, with no small surprise on his countenance.—"Why, yes," answered the other, "the Sultan and I; do you know me? I am the Chan of Tartary."

Harley was a good deal struck by this discovery; he had prudence enough, however, to conceal his amazement, and bowing as low to the monarch as his dignity required, left him immediately, and joined his companions.

He found them in a quarter of the house set apart for the insane of the other sex, several of whom had gathered about the female visitors, and were examining, with rather more accuracy than might have been expected, the particulars of their dress.

Separate from the rest stood one whose appearance had something of superior dignity. Her face, though pale and wasted, was less squalid than those of the others, and showed a dejection of that decent kind, which moves our pity unmixed with horror: upon her, therefore, the eyes of all were immediately turned. The keeper who accompanied them observed it: " This," said he, " is a young lady who was born to ride in her coach and six. She was beloved, if the story I have heard is true, by a young gentleman, her equal in birth, though by no means her match in fortune: but love, they say, is blind, and so she fancied him as much as he did her. Her father, it seems, would not hear of their marriage, and threatened to turn her out of doors if ever she saw him again. Upon this the young gentleman took a voyage to the West Indies, in hopes of bettering his fortune, and obtaining his mistress; but he was scarce landed, when he was seized with one of the fevers which are common in those islands, and died in a few days, lamented by every one that knew him. This news soon reached his mistress, who was at the same time pressed by her father to marry a rich miserly fellow, who was old enough to be her grandfather. The death of her lover had no effect on her inhuman parent: he was only the more earnest for her marriage with the man he had provided for her; and what between her despair at the death of the one, and her aversion to the other, the poor young lady was reduced to the condition you see her in. But God would not prosper such cruelty; her father's affairs soon after went to wreck, and he died almost a beggar."

Though this story was told in very plain language, it had particularly attracted Harley's notice; he had given it the tribute of some tears. The unfortunate young lady had till now seemed entranced in thought, with her eyes fixed on a little garnet ring she wore on her finger; she turned them now upon Harley. " My Billy is no more! " said she; " do you weep for my Billy? Blessings on your tears! I would weep too, but my brain is dry; and it burns, it burns, it burns! "— She drew nearer to Harley.—" Be comforted, young lady," said he, " your Billy is in heaven."—" Is he, indeed? and shall we meet again? and shall that frightful man (pointing to the keeper) not be there?—Alas! I am grown naughty of late; I have almost forgotten to think of heaven: yet I pray some- times; when I can, I pray; and sometimes I sing; when I am saddest, I sing:—You shall hear me—hush!

" Light be the earth on Billy's breast,
    And green the sod that wraps his grave."

There was a plaintive wildness in the air not to be withstood; and, except the keeper's, there was not an unmoistened eye around her.

" Do you weep again?" said she. " I would not have you weep: you are like my Billy; you are, believe me; just so he looked when he gave me this ring; poor Billy! 'twas the last time ever we met!—

" 'Twas when the seas were roaring—I love you for resembling my Billy; but I shall never love any man like him." —She stretched out her hand to Harley; he pressed it between both of his, and bathed it with his tears.—" Nay, that is Billy's ring," said she, " you cannot have it, indeed; but here is another, look here, which I plated to-day of some gold-thread from this bit of stuff; will you keep it for my sake? I am a strange girl; but my heart is harmless: my poor heart; it will burst some day; feel how it beats!" She pressed his hand to her bosom, then holding her head in the attitude of listening —" Hark! one, two, three! be quiet, thou little trembler; my Billy is cold!—but I had forgotten the ring."—She put it on his finger.—" Farewell! I must leave you now."—She would have withdrawn her hand; Harley held it to his lips.—" I dare not stay longer; my head throbs sadly: farewell!"—— She walked with a hurried step to a little apartment at some distance. Harley stood fixed in astonishment and pity: his friend gave money to the keeper.—Harley looked on his ring. —He put a couple of guineas into the man's hand: " Be kind to that unfortunate "—He burst into tears, and left them.

———

CHAPTER XXI

THE MISANTHROPIST

THE friend who had conducted him to Moorfields called upon him again the next evening. After some talk on the adventures of the preceding day: " I carried you yesterday," said he to Harley, " to visit the mad; let me introduce you to-night, at supper, to one of the wise: but you must not look for anything of the Socratic pleasantry about him; on the contrary, I warn you to expect the spirit of a Diogenes.

That you may be a little prepared for his extraordinary manner, I will let you into some particulars of his history.

"He is the elder of the two sons of a gentleman of considerable estate in the country. Their father died when they were young: both were remarkable at school for quickness of parts and extent of genius; this had been bred to no profession, because his father's fortune, which descended to him, was thought sufficient to set him above it; the other was put apprentice to an eminent attorney. In this the expectations of his friends were more consulted than his own inclination; for both his brother and he had feelings of that warm kind that could ill brook a study so dry as the law, especially in that department of it which was allotted to him. But the difference of their tempers made the characteristical distinction between them. The younger, from the gentleness of his nature, bore with patience a situation entirely discordant to his genius and disposition. At times, indeed, his pride would suggest of how little importance those talents were which the partiality of his friends had often extolled: they were now incumbrances in a walk of life where the dull and the ignorant passed him at every turn; his fancy and his feeling were invincible obstacles to eminence in a situation where his fancy had no room for exertion, and his feeling experienced perpetual disgust. But these murmurings he never suffered to be heard; and that he might not offend the prudence of those who had been concerned in the choice of his profession, he continued to labour in it several years, till, by the death of a relation, he succeeded to an estate of a little better than £100 a year, with which, and the small patrimony left him, he retired into the country, and made a love-match with a young lady of a similar temper to his own, with whom the sagacious world pitied him for finding happiness.

"But his elder brother, whom you are to see at supper, if you will do us the favour of your company, was naturally impetuous, decisive, and overbearing. He entered into life with those ardent expectations by which young men are commonly deluded: in his friendships, warm to excess; and equally violent in his dislikes. He was on the brink of marriage with a young lady, when one of those friends, for whose honour he would have pawned his life, made an elopement with that very goddess, and left him besides deeply engaged for sums which that good friend's extravagance had squandered.

"The dreams he had formerly enjoyed were now changed for ideas of a very different nature. He abjured all confidence in anything of human form; sold his lands, which still produced him a very large reversion, came to town, and immured himself, with a woman who had been his nurse, in little better than a garret; and has ever since applied his talents to the vilifying of his species. In one thing I must take the liberty to instruct you; however different your sentiments may be (and different they must be), you will suffer him to go on without contradiction; otherwise, he will be silent immediately, and we shall not get a word from him all the night after." Harley promised to remember this injunction, and accepted the invitation of his friend.

When they arrived at the house, they were informed that the gentleman was come, and had been shown into the parlour. They found him sitting with a daughter of his friend's, about three years old, on his knee, whom he was teaching the alphabet from a horn book: at a little distance stood a sister of hers, some years older. "Get you away, miss," said he to this last; "you are a pert gossip, and I will have nothing to do with you."—"Nay," answered she, "Nancy is your favourite; you are quite in love with Nancy."—"Take away that girl," said he to her father, whom he now observed to have entered the room; "she has woman about her already." The children were accordingly dismissed.

Betwixt that and supper-time he did not utter a syllable. When supper came, he quarrelled with every dish at table, but eat of them all; only exempting from his censures a salad, "which you have not spoiled," said he, "because you have not attempted to cook it."

When the wine was set upon the table, he took from his pocket a particular smoking apparatus, and filled his pipe, without taking any more notice of Harley, or his friend, than if no such persons had been in the room.

Harley could not help stealing a look of surprise at him; but his friend, who knew his humour, returned it by annihilating his presence in the like manner, and, leaving him to his own meditations, addressed himself entirely to Harley.

In their discourse some mention happened to be made of an amiable character, and the words *honour* and *politeness* were applied to it. Upon this, the gentleman, laying down his pipe, and changing the tone of his countenance, from an ironical grin to something more intently contemptuous: "Honour," said he: "Honour and Politeness! this is the coin of the world, and passes current with the fools of it. You have substituted the shadow Honour, instead of the substance Virtue; and have banished the reality of friendship for the fictitious semblance which you have termed Politeness: politeness, which consists in a certain ceremonious jargon, more ridiculous to the ear of reason than the voice of a puppet. You have invented sounds, which you worship, though they tyrannize over your peace; and are surrounded with empty forms, which take from the honest emotions of joy, and add to the poignancy of misfortune." " Sir!" said Harley—his friend winked to him, to remind him of the caution he had received. He was silenced by the thought. The philosopher turned his eye upon him: he examined him from top to toe, with a sort of triumphant contempt. Harley's coat happened to be a new one; the other's was as shabby as could possibly be supposed to be on the back of a gentleman: there was much significance in his look with regard to this coat; it spoke of the sleekness of folly and the threadbareness of wisdom.

" Truth," continued he, " the most amiable, as well as the most natural of virtues, you are at pains to eradicate. Your very nurseries are seminaries of falsehood; and what is called Fashion in manhood completes the system of avowed insincerity. Mankind, in the gross, is a gaping monster, that loves to be deceived, and has seldom been disappointed: nor is their vanity less fallacious to your philosophers, who adopt modes of truth to follow them through the paths of error, and defend paradoxes merely to be singular in defending them. These are they whom ye term Ingenious; 'tis a phrase of commendation I detest: it implies an attempt to impose on my judgment, by flattering my imagination; yet these are they whose works are read by the old with delight, which the young are taught to look upon as the codes of knowledge and philosophy.

" Indeed, the education of your youth is every way preposterous; you waste at school years in improving talents, without having ever spent an hour in discovering them; one promiscuous line of instruction is followed, without regard to genius, capacity, or probable situation in the commonwealth. From this bear-garden of the pedagogue, a raw, unprincipled boy is turned loose upon the world to travel; without any ideas but those of improving his dress at Paris, or starting into taste by gazing on some paintings at Rome. Ask him of the manners of the people, and he will tell you that the skirt is worn much shorter in France, and that everybody eats macaroni in Italy. When he returns home, he buys a seat in parliament, and studies the constitution at Arthur's.

" Nor are your females trained to any more useful purpose: they are taught, by the very rewards which their nurses propose for good behaviour, by the first thing like a jest which they hear from every male visitor of the family, that a young woman is a creature to be married; and when they are grown somewhat older, are instructed that it is the purpose of marriage to have the enjoyment of pin-money, and the expectation of a jointure."

[1] " These, indeed, are the effects of luxury, which is, perhaps, inseparable from a certain degree of power and grandeur in a nation. But it is not simply of the progress of luxury that we have to complain: did its votaries keep in their own sphere of thoughtless dissipation, we might despise them without emotion; but the frivolous pursuits of pleasure are mingled with the most important concerns of the state; and public enterprise shall sleep till he who should guide its operation has decided his bets at Newmarket, or fulfilled his engagement with a favourite mistress in the country. We want some man of acknowledged eminence to point our counsels with that firmness which the counsels of a great people require. We have hundreds of ministers, who press forward into office

[1] Though the Curate could not remember having shown this chapter to anybody, I strongly suspect that these political observations are the work of a later pen than the rest of this performance. There seems to have been, by some accident, a gap in the manuscript, from the words, " Expectation of a jointure," to these, " In short, man is an animal," where the present blank ends; and some other person (for the hand is different, and the ink whiter) has filled part of it with sentiments of his own. Whoever he was, he seems to have caught some portion of the spirit of the man he personates.

without having ever learned that art which is necessary for every business: the art of thinking; and mistake the petulance, which could give inspiration to smart sarcasms on an obnoxious measure in a popular assembly, for the ability which is to balance the interest of kingdoms, and investigate the latent sources of national superiority. With the administration of such men the people can never be satisfied; for besides that their confidence is gained only by the view of superior talents, there needs that depth of knowledge, which is not only acquainted with the just extent of power, but can also trace its connection with the expedient, to preserve its possessors from the contempt which attends irresolution, or the resentment which follows temerity."

*   *   *   *   *   *

[Here a considerable part is wanting.]

* * "In short, man is an animal equally selfish and vain. Vanity, indeed, is but a modification of selfishness. From the latter, there are some who pretend to be free: they are generally such as declaim against the lust of wealth and power, because they have never been able to attain any high degree in either: they boast of generosity and feeling. They tell us (perhaps they tell us in rhyme) that the sensations of an honest heart, of a mind universally benevolent, make up the quiet bliss which they enjoy; but they will not, by this, be exempted from the charge of selfishness. Whence the luxurious happiness they describe in their little family-circles? Whence the pleasure which they feel, when they trim their evening fires, and listen to the howl of winter's wind? Whence, but from the secret reflection of what houseless wretches feel from it? Or do you administer comfort in affliction—the motive is at hand; I have had it preached to me in nineteen out of twenty of your consolatory discourses—the comparative littleness of our own misfortunes.

"With vanity your best virtues are grossly tainted: your benevolence, which ye deduce immediately from the natural impulse of the heart, squints to it for its reward. There are some, indeed, who tell us of the satisfaction which flows from a secret consciousness of good actions: this secret satisfaction is truly excellent—when we have some friend to whom we may discover its excellence."

He now paused a moment to re-light his pipe, when a clock, that stood at his back, struck eleven; he started up at the sound, took his hat and his cane, and nodding good night with his head, walked out of the room. The gentleman of the house called a servant to bring the stranger's surtout. "What sort of a night is it, fellow?" said he.—"It rains, sir," answered the servant, "with an easterly wind."—"Easterly for ever!" He made no other reply; but shrugging up his shoulders till they almost touched his ears, wrapped himself tight in his great coat, and disappeared.

"This is a strange creature," said his friend to Harley. "I cannot say," answered he, "that his remarks are of the pleasant kind: it is curious to observe how the nature of truth may be changed by the garb it wears; softened to the admonition of friendship, or soured into the severity of reproof: yet this severity may be useful to some tempers; it somewhat resembles a file: disagreeable in its operation, but hard metals may be the brighter for it."

*   *   *   *   *   *

CHAPTER XXV

HIS SKILL IN PHYSIOGNOMY

THE company at the baronet's removed to the play-house accordingly, and Harley took his usual route into the Park. He observed, as he entered, a fresh-looking elderly gentleman in conversation with a beggar, who, leaning on his crutch, was recounting the hardships he had undergone, and explaining the wretchedness of his present condition. This was a very interesting dialogue to Harley; he was rude enough, therefore, to slacken his pace as he approached, and at last to make a full stop at the gentleman's back, who was just then expressing his compassion for the beggar, and regretting that he had not a farthing of change about him. At saying this, he looked piteously on the fellow: there was something in his physiognomy which caught Harley's notice: indeed, physiognomy was one of Harley's foibles, for which he had been often rebuked by his aunt in the country, who used to tell him that when he was come to her years and experience he would know that all's not gold that glisters : and it must be owned that his aunt was a very sensible, harsh-looking maiden lady of threescore and upwards.   But he was too apt to forget this caution; and now, it seems, it had not occurred to him.   Stepping up, therefore, to the gentleman, who was lamenting the want of silver, " Your intentions, sir," said he, " are so good, that I cannot help lending you my assistance to carry them into execution," and gave the beggar a shilling.   The other returned a suitable compliment, and extolled the benevolence of Harley.   They kept walking together, and benevolence grew the topic of discourse.

The stranger was fluent on the subject.   " There is no use of money," said he, " equal to that of beneficence.   With the profuse, it is lost; and even with those who lay it out according to the prudence of the world, the objects acquired by it pall on the sense, and have scarce become our own till they lose their value with the power of pleasing; but here the enjoyment grows on reflection, and our money is most truly ours when it ceases being in our possession."

" Yet I agree in some measure," answered Harley, " with those who think that charity to our common beggars is often misplaced;   there are objects less obtrusive whose title is a better one."

" We cannot easily distinguish," said the stranger;   " and even of the worthless, are there not many whose imprudence, or whose vice, may have been one dreadful consequence of misfortune? "

Harley looked again in his face, and blessed himself for his skill in physiognomy.

By this time they had reached the end of the walk, the old gentleman leaning on the rails to take breath, and in the meantime they were joined by a younger man, whose figure was much above the appearance of his dress, which was poor and shabby.   Harley's former companion addressed him as an acquaintance, and they turned on the walk together.

The elder of the strangers complained of the closeness of the evening, and asked the other if he would go with him into a house hard by, and take one draught of excellent cider. " The man who keeps this house," said he to Harley, " was once a servant of mine. I could not think of turning loose upon the world a faithful old fellow, for no other reason but that his age had incapacitated him; so I gave him an annuity of ten pounds, with the help of which he has set up this little place here, and his daughter goes and sells milk in the city, while her father manages his tap-room, as he calls it, at home. I can't well ask a gentleman of your appearance to accompany me to so paltry a place." "Sir," replied Harley, interrupting him, "I would much rather enter it than the most celebrated tavern in town. To give to the necessitous may sometimes be a weakness in the man; to encourage industry is a duty in the citizen." They entered the house accordingly.

On a table at the corner of the room lay a pack of cards, loosely thrown together. The old gentleman reproved the man of the house for encouraging so idle an amusement. Harley attempted to defend him from the necessity of accommodating himself to the humour of his guests, and taking up the cards, began to shuffle them backwards and forwards in his hand. "Nay, I don't think cards so unpardonable an amusement as some do," replied the other; "and now and then, about this time of the evening, when my eyes begin to fail me for my book, I divert myself with a game at piquet, without finding my morals a bit relaxed by it. Do you play piquet, sir?" (to Harley.) Harley answered in the affirmative; upon which the other proposed playing a pool at a shilling the game, doubling the stakes; adding, that he never played higher with anybody.

Harley's good nature could not refuse the benevolent old man; and the younger stranger, though he at first pleaded prior engagements, yet being earnestly solicited by his friend, at last yielded to solicitation.

When they began to play, the old gentleman, somewhat to the surprise of Harley, produced ten shillings to serve for markers of his score. "He had no change for the beggar," said Harley to himself; "but I can easily account for it; it is curious to observe the affection that inanimate things will create in us by a long acquaintance. If I may judge from my own feelings, the old man would not part with one of these counters for ten times its intrinsic value; it even got the better of his benevolence! I, myself, have a pair of old brass sleeve buttons." Here he was interrupted by being told that the old gentleman had beat the younger, and that it was his turn to take up the conqueror. "Your game has been short," said Harley. "I re-piqued him," answered the old man, with joy sparkling in his countenance. Harley wished to be re-piqued too, but he was disappointed; for he had the same good fortune against his opponent. Indeed, never did fortune, mutable as she is, delight in mutability so much as at that moment. The victory was so quick, and so constantly alternate, that the stake, in a short time, amounted to no less a sum than £12, Harley's proportion of which was within half-a-guinea of the money he had in his pocket. He had before proposed a division, but the old gentleman opposed it with such a pleasant warmth in his manner, that it was always over-ruled. Now, however, he told them that he had an appointment with some gentlemen, and it was within a few minutes of his hour. The young stranger had gained one game, and was engaged in the second with the other; they agreed, therefore, that the stake should be divided, if the old gentleman won that: which was more than probable, as his score was 90 to 35, and he was elder hand; but a momentous re-pique decided it in favour of his adversary, who seemed to enjoy his victory mingled with regret, for having won too much, while his friend, with great ebullience of passion, many praises of his own good play, and many maledictions on the power of chance, took up the cards, and threw them into the fire.

CHAPTER XXVI

THE MAN OF FEELING IN A BROTHEL

THE company he was engaged to meet were assembled in Fleet Street. He had walked some time along the Strand, amidst a crowd of those wretches who wait the uncertain wages of prostitution, with ideas of pity suitable to the scene around him and the feelings he possessed, and had got as far as Somerset House, when one of them laid hold of his arm, and, with a voice tremulous and faint, asked him for a pint of wine, in a manner more supplicatory than is usual with those whom the infamy of their profession has deprived of shame. He turned round at the demand, and looked steadfastly on the person who made it.

She was above the common size, and elegantly formed; her face was thin and hollow, and showed the remains of tarnished beauty. Her eyes were black, but had little of their lustre left; her cheeks had some paint laid on without art, and productive of no advantage to her complexion, which exhibited a deadly paleness on the other parts of her face.

Harley stood in the attitude of hesitation; which she, interpreting to her advantage, repeated her request, and endeavoured to force a leer of invitation into her countenance. He took her arm, and they walked on to one of those obsequious taverns in the neighbourhood, where the dearness of the wine is a discharge in full for the character of the house. From what impulse he did this we do not mean to enquire; as it has ever been against our nature to search for motives where bad ones are to be found. They entered, and a waiter showed them a room, and placed a bottle of wine on the table.

Harley filled the lady's glass: which she had no sooner tasted, than dropping it on the floor, and eagerly catching his arm, her eye grew fixed, her lip assumed a clayey whiteness, and she fell back lifeless in her chair.

Harley started from his seat, and, catching her in his arms, supported her from falling to the ground, looking wildly at the door, as if he wanted to run for assistance, but durst not leave the miserable creature. It was not till some minutes after that it occurred to him to ring the bell, which at last, however, he thought of, and rung with repeated violence even after the waiter appeared. Luckily the waiter had his senses somewhat more about him; and snatching up a bottle of water, which stood on a buffet at the end of the room, he sprinkled it over the hands and face of the dying figure before him. She began to revive, and, with the assistance of some hartshorn drops, which Harley now for the first time drew from his pocket, was able to desire the waiter to bring her a crust of bread, of which she swallowed some mouthfuls with the appearance of the keenest hunger. The waiter withdrew: when turning to Harley, sobbing at the same time, and shedding tears, "I am sorry, sir," said she, "that I should have given you so much trouble; but you will pity me when I tell you that till now I have not tasted a morsel these two days past."—He fixed his eyes on hers—every circumstance but the last was forgotten; and he took her hand with as much respect as if she had been a duchess. It was ever the privilege of misfortune to be revered by him.—" Two days!" said he; "and I have fared sumptuously every day!"—He was reaching to the bell; she understood his meaning, and prevented him. " I beg, sir," said she, "that you would give yourself no more trouble about a wretch who does not wish to live; but, at present, I could not eat a bit; my stomach even rose at the last mouthful of that crust."—He offered to call a chair, saying that he hoped a little rest would relieve her.—He had one half-guinea left. " I am sorry," he said, "that at present I should be able to make you an offer of no more than this paltry sum."—She burst into tears: " Your generosity, sir, is abused; to bestow it on me is to take it from the virtuous. I have no title but misery to plead: misery of my own procuring." " No more of that," answered Harley; "there is virtue in these tears; let the fruit of them be virtue."—He rung, and ordered a chair.—" Though I am the vilest of beings," said she, " I have not forgotten every virtue; gratitude, I hope, I shall still have left, did I but know who is my benefactor."—" My name is Harley."—" Could I ever have an opportunity?"—" You shall, and a glorious one too! your future conduct—but I do not mean to reproach you—if, I say —it will be the noblest reward—I will do myself the pleasure of seeing you again."—Here the waiter entered, and told them the chair was at the door; the lady informed Harley of her lodgings, and he promised to wait on her at ten next morning.

He led her to the chair, and returned to clear with the waiter, without ever once reflecting that he had no money in his pocket. He was ashamed to make an excuse; yet an excuse must be made: he was beginning to frame one, when the waiter cut him short by telling him that he could not run scores; but that, if he would leave his watch, or any other pledge, it would be as safe as if it lay in his pocket. Harley jumped at the proposal, and pulling out his watch, delivered it into his hands immediately, and having, for once, had the precaution to take a note of the lodging he intended to visit next morning, sallied forth with a blush of triumph on his face, without taking notice of the sneer of the waiter, who, twirling the watch in his hand, made him a profound bow at the door, and whispered to a girl, who stood in the passage, something, in which the word CULLY was honoured with a particular emphasis.

——

CHAPTER XXVII

HIS SKILL IN PHYSIOGNOMY IS DOUBTED

AFTER he had been some time with the company he had appointed to meet, and the last bottle was called for, he first recollected that he would be again at a loss how to discharge his share of the reckoning. He applied, therefore, to one of them, with whom he was most intimate, acknowledging that he had not a farthing of money about him; and, upon being jocularly asked the reason, acquainted them with the two adventures we have just now related. One of the company asked him if the old man in Hyde Park did not wear a brownish coat, with a narrow gold edging, and his companion an old green frock, with a buff-coloured waistcoat. Upon Harley's recollecting that they did, "Then," said he, "you may be thankful you have come off so well; they are two as noted sharpers, in their way, as any in town, and but t'other night took me in for a much larger sum. I had some thoughts of applying to a justice, but one does not like to be seen in those matters."

Harley answered, "That he could not but fancy the gentleman was mistaken, as he never saw a face promise more honesty than that of the old man he had met with."—"His face!" said a grave-looking man, who sat opposite to him, squirting the juice of his tobacco obliquely into the grate. There was something very emphatical in the action, for it was followed by a burst of laughter round the table. "Gentlemen," said Harley, "you are disposed to be merry; it may be as you imagine, for I confess myself ignorant of the town; but there is one thing which makes me bear the loss of my money with temper: the young fellow who won it must have been miserably poor; I observed him borrow money for the stake from his friend: he had distress and hunger in his countenance: be his character what it may, his necessities at least plead for him." At this there was a louder laugh than before. "Gentlemen," said the lawyer, one of whose conversations with Harley we have already recorded, "here's a very pretty fellow for you! to have heard him talk some nights ago, as I did, you might have sworn he was a saint; yet now he games with sharpers, and loses his money, and is bubbled by a fine story invented by a whore, and pawns his watch; here are sanctified doings with a witness!"

"Young gentleman," said his friend on the other side of the table, "let me advise you to be a little more cautious for the future; and as for faces—you may look into them to know whether a man's nose be a long or a short one."

CHAPTER XXVIII

HE KEEPS HIS APPOINTMENT

THE last night's raillery of his companions was recalled to his remembrance when he awoke, and the colder homilies of prudence began to suggest some things which were nowise favourable for a performance of his promise to the unfortunate female he had met with before. He rose, uncertain of his purpose; but the torpor of such considerations was seldom prevalent over the warmth of his nature. He walked some turns backwards and forwards in his room; he recalled the languid form of the fainting wretch to his mind; he wept at the recollection of her tears. "Though I am the vilest of beings, I have not forgotten every virtue; gratitude, I hope, I shall still have left."—He took a larger stride— "Powers of mercy that surround me!" cried he, "do ye not smile upon deeds like these? to calculate the chances of deception is too tedious a business for the life of man!"—The clock struck ten.—When he had got down-stairs, he found that he had forgot the note of her lodgings; he gnawed his lips at the delay: he was fairly on the pavement, when he recollected having left his purse; he did but just prevent himself from articulating an imprecation. He rushed a second time up into his chamber. "What a wretch I am!" said he; "ere this time, perhaps——" 'Twas a perhaps not to be borne;—two vibrations of a pendulum would have served him to lock his bureau; but they could not be spared.

When he reached the house, and inquired for Miss Atkins (for that was the lady's name), he was shown up three pair of stairs, into a small room lighted by one narrow lattice, and patched round with shreds of different-coloured paper. In the darkest corner stood something like a bed, before which a tattered coverlet hung by way of curtain. He had not waited long when she appeared. Her face had the glister of new-washed tears on it. "I am ashamed, sir," said she, "that you should have taken this fresh piece of trouble about one so little worthy of it; but, to the humane, I know there is a pleasure in goodness for its own sake: if you have patience for the recital of my story, it may palliate, though it cannot excuse, my faults." Harley bowed, as a sign of assent; and she began as follows:—

"I am the daughter of an officer, whom a service of forty years had advanced no higher than the rank of captain. I have had hints from himself, and been informed by others, that it was in some measure owing to those principles of rigid honour, which it was his boast to possess, and which he early inculcated on me, that he had been able to arrive at no better station. My mother died when I was a child: old enough to grieve for her death, but incapable of remembering her precepts. Though my father was dotingly fond of her, yet there were some sentiments in which they materially differed: she had been bred from her infancy in the strictest principles of religion, and took the morality of her conduct from the motives which an adherence to those principles suggested. My father, who had been in the army from his youth, affixed an idea of pusillanimity to that virtue, which was formed by the doctrines, excited by the rewards, or guarded by the terrors of revelation; his darling idol was the honour of a soldier: a term which he held in such reverence, that he used it for his most sacred asseveration. When my mother died, I was some time suffered to continue in those sentiments which her instructions had produced; but soon after, though, from respect to her memory, my father did not absolutely ridicule them, yet he showed, in his discourse to others, so little regard to them, and at times suggested to me motives of action so different, that I was soon weaned from opinions which I began to consider as the dreams of superstition, or the artful inventions of designing hypocrisy. My mother's books were left behind at the different quarters we removed to, and my reading was principally confined to plays, novels, and those poetical descriptions of the beauty of virtue and honour, which the circulating libraries easily afforded.

" As I was generally reckoned handsome, and the quickness of my parts extolled by all our visitors, my father had a pride in showing me to the world. I was young, giddy, open to adulation, and vain of those talents which acquired it.

" After the last war, my father was reduced to half-pay; with which we retired to a village in the country, which the acquaintance of some genteel families who resided in it, and the cheapness of living, particularly recommended. My father rented a small house, with a piece of ground sufficient to keep a horse for him, and a cow for the benefit of his family. An old man servant managed his ground; while a maid, who had formerly been my mother's, and had since been mine, undertook the care of our little dairy: they were assisted in each of their provinces by my father and me; and we passed our time in a state of tranquillity, which he had always talked of with delight, and which my train of reading had taught me to admire.

" Though I had never seen the polite circles of the metropolis, the company my father had introduced me into had given me a degree of good breeding, which soon discovered a superiority over the young ladies of our village. I was quoted as an example of politeness, and my company courted by most of the considerable families in the neighbourhood.

" Amongst the houses to which I was frequently invited was Sir George Winbrooke's. He had two daughters nearly of my age, with whom, though they had been bred up in those maxims of vulgar doctrine which my superior understanding could not but despise, yet as their good nature led them to an imitation of my manners in everything else, I cultivated a particular friendship.

" Some months after our first acquaintance, Sir George's eldest son came home from his travels. His figure, his ad-

THE MAN OF FEELING

dress, and conversation, were not unlike those warm ideas of
an accomplished man which my favourite novels had taught
me to form; and his sentiments on the article of religion were
as liberal as my own: when any of these happened to be the
topic of our discourse, I, who before had been silent, from a
fear of being single in opposition, now kindled at the fire he
raised, and defended our mutual opinions with all the eloquence I was mistress of. He would be respectfully attentive
all the while; and when I had ended, would raise his eyes from
the ground, look at me with a gaze of admiration, and express
his applause in the highest strain of encomium. This was an
incense the more pleasing, as I seldom or never had met with
it before; for the young gentlemen who visited Sir George
were for the most part of that common race of country squires,
the pleasure of whose lives is derived from fox-hunting: these
are seldom solicitous to please the women at all; or if they
were, would never think of applying their flattery to the mind.

"Mr. Winbrooke observed the weakness of my soul, and
took every occasion of improving the esteem he had gained.
He asked my opinion of every author, of every sentiment,
with that submissive diffidence, which showed an unlimited
confidence in my understanding. I saw myself revered, as
a superior being, by one whose judgment my vanity told me
was not likely to err: preferred by him to all the other visitors
of my sex, whose fortunes and rank should have entitled them
to a much higher degree of notice: I saw their little jealousies
at the distinguished attention he paid me; it was gratitude, it
was pride, it was love! Love which had made too fatal a
progress in my heart, before any declaration on his part
should have warranted a return: but I interpreted every look
of attention, every expression of compliment, to the passion
I imagined him inspired with, and imputed to his sensibility
that silence which was the effect of art and design. At length,
however, he took an opportunity of declaring his love: he now
expressed himself in such ardent terms, that prudence might
have suspected their sincerity: but prudence is rarely found
in the situation I had been unguardedly led into; besides, that
the course of reading to which I had been accustomed, did
not lead me to conclude, that his expressions could be too
warm to be sincere: nor was I even alarmed at the manner

in which he talked of marriage, a subjection, he often hinted, to which genuine love should scorn to be confined. The woman, he would often say, who had merit like mine to fix his affection, could easily command it for ever. That honour too which I revered, was often called in to enforce his sentiments. I did not, however, absolutely assent to them; but I found my regard for their opposites diminish by degrees. If it is dangerous to be convinced, it is dangerous to listen; for our reason is so much of a machine, that it will not always be able to resist, when the ear is perpetually assailed.

"In short, Mr. Harley (for I tire you with a relation, the catastrophe of which you will already have imagined), I fell a prey to his artifices. He had not been able so thoroughly to convert me, that my conscience was silent on the subject; but he was so assiduous to give repeated proofs of unabated affection, that I hushed its suggestions as they rose. The world, however, I knew, was not to be silenced; and therefore I took occasion to express my uneasiness to my seducer, and entreat him, as he valued the peace of one to whom he professed such attachment, to remove it by a marriage. He made excuses from his dependence on the will of his father, but quieted my fears by the promise of endeavouring to win his assent.

" My father had been some days absent on a visit to a dying relation, from whom he had considerable expectations. I was left at home, with no other company than my books: my books I found were not now such companions as they used to be; I was restless, melancholy, unsatisfied with myself. But judge my situation when I received a billet from Mr. Winbrooke informing me, that he had sounded Sir George on the subject we had talked of, and found him so averse to any match so unequal to his own rank and fortune, that he was obliged, with whatever reluctance, to bid adieu to a place, the remembrance of which should ever be dear to him.

" I read this letter a hundred times over. Alone, helpless, conscious of guilt, and abandoned by every better thought, my mind was one motley scene of terror, confusion, and remorse. A thousand expedients suggested themselves, and a thousand fears told me they would be vain: at last, in an agony of despair, I packed up a few clothes, took what money and trinkets were in the house, and set out for London, whither I understood he was gone; pretending to my maid, that I had received letters from my father requiring my immediate attendance. I had no other companion than a boy, a servant to the man from whom I hired my horses. I arrived in London within an hour of Mr. Winbrooke, and accidentally alighted at the very inn where he was.

"He started and turned pale when he saw me; but recovered himself in time enough to make many new protestations of regard, and beg me to make myself easy under a disappointment which was equally afflicting to him. He procured me lodgings, where I slept, or rather endeavoured to sleep, for that night. Next morning I saw him again, he then mildly observed on the imprudence of my precipitate flight from the country, and proposed my removing to lodgings at another end of the town, to elude the search of my father, till he should fall upon some method of excusing my conduct to him, and reconciling him to my return. We took a hackney-coach, and drove to the house he mentioned.

"It was situated in a dirty lane, furnished with a tawdry affectation of finery, with some old family pictures hanging on walls which their own cobwebs would better have suited. I was struck with a secret dread at entering, nor was it lessened by the appearance of the landlady, who had that look of selfish shrewdness, which, of all others, is the most hateful to those whose feelings are untinctured with the world. A girl, who she told us was her niece, sat by her, playing on a guitar, while herself was at work, with the assistance of spectacles, and had a prayer-book with the leaves folded down in several places, lying on the table before her. Perhaps, sir, I tire you with my minuteness, but the place, and every circumstance about it, is so impressed on my mind, that I shall never forget it.

"I dined that day with Mr. Winbrooke alone. He lost by degrees that restraint which I perceived too well to hang about him before, and, with his former gaiety and good humour, repeated the flattering things which, though they had once been fatal, I durst not now distrust. At last, taking my hand and kissing it, 'It is thus,' said he, 'that love will last, while freedom is preserved; thus let us ever be blessed, without the galling thought that we are tied to a condition where we may cease to be so.'

"I answered, 'That the world thought otherwise: that it had certain ideas of good fame, which it was impossible not to wish to maintain.'

"'The world,' said he, 'is a tyrant, they are slaves who obey it; let us be happy without the pale of the world. To-morrow I shall leave this quarter of it, for one where the talkers of the world shall be foiled, and lose us. Could not my Emily accompany me? my friend, my companion, the mistress of my soul! Nay, do not look so, Emily! Your father may grieve for a while, but your father shall be taken care of; this bank-bill I intend as the comfort for his daughter.'

"I could contain myself no longer: 'Wretch,' I exclaimed, 'dost thou imagine that my father's heart could brook dependence on the destroyer of his child, and tamely accept of a base equivalent for her honour and his own?'

"'Honour, my Emily,' said he, 'is the word of fools, or of those wiser men who cheat them. 'Tis a fantastic bauble that does not suit the gravity of your father's age; but, whatever it is, I am afraid it can never be perfectly restored to you: exchange the word then, and let pleasure be your object now.'

"At these words he clasped me in his arms, and pressed his lips rudely to my bosom. I started from my seat. 'Perfidious villain!' said I, 'who dar'st insult the weakness thou hast undone; were that father here, thy coward soul would shrink from the vengeance of his honour! Cursed be that wretch who has deprived him of it! oh! doubly cursed, who has dragged on his hoary head the infamy which should have crushed her own!' I snatched a knife which lay beside me, and would have plunged it in my breast, but the monster prevented my purpose, and smiling with a grin of barbarous insult—

"'Madam,' said he, 'I confess you are too much in heroics for me; I am sorry we should differ about trifles: but as I seem somehow to have offended you, I would willingly remedy it by taking my leave. You have been put to some foolish expense in this journey on my account; allow me to reimburse you.'

"So saying he laid a bank-bill, of what amount I had no patience to see, upon the table. Shame, grief, and indignation choked my utterance; unable to speak my wrongs, and unable to bear them in silence, I fell in a swoon at his feet.

"What happened in the interval I cannot tell, but when I came to myself I was in the arms of the landlady, with her niece chafing my temples, and doing all in her power for my recovery. She had much compassion in her countenance; the old woman assumed the softest look she was capable of, and both endeavoured to bring me comfort. They continued to show me many civilities, and even the aunt began to be less disagreeable in my sight. To the wretched, to the forlorn, as I was, small offices of kindness are endearing.

"Meantime my money was far spent, nor did I attempt to conceal my wants from their knowledge. I had frequent thoughts of returning to my father; but the dread of a life of scorn is insurmountable. I avoided, therefore, going abroad when I had a chance of being seen by any former acquaintance, nor indeed did my health for a great while permit it; and suffered the old woman, at her own suggestion, to call me niece at home, where we now and then saw (when they could prevail on me to leave my room) one or two other elderly women, and sometimes a grave business-like man, who showed great compassion for my indisposition, and made me very obligingly an offer of a room at his country-house for the recovery of my health. This offer I did not choose to accept, but told my landlady, 'that I should be glad to be employed in any way of business which my skill in needle-work could recommend me to, confessing, at the same time, that I was afraid I should scarce be able to pay her what I already owed for board and lodging, and that for her other good offices, I had nothing but thanks to give her.'

"'My dear child,' said she, 'do not talk of paying; since I lost my own sweet girl' (here she wept), 'your very picture she was, Miss Emily, I have nobody, except my niece, to whom I should leave any little thing I have been able to save; you shall live with me, my dear; and I have sometimes a little millinery work, in which, when you are inclined to it, you may assist us. By the way, here are a pair of ruffles we have just finished for that gentleman you saw here at tea; a distant relation of mine, and a worthy man he is. 'Twas pity you refused the offer of an apartment at his country house; my niece, you know, was to have accompanied you, and you might have fancied yourself at home; a most sweet place it is, and but a short mile beyond Hampstead. Who knows, Miss Emily, what effect such a visit might have had! If I had half your beauty I should not waste it pining after e'er a worthless fellow of them all.'

" I felt my heart swell at her words; I would have been angry if I could, but I was in that stupid state which is not easily awakened to anger: when I would have chid her the reproof stuck in my throat; I could only weep!

" Her want of respect increased, as I had not spirit to assert it. My work was now rather imposed than offered, and I became a drudge for the bread I eat: but my dependence and servility grew in proportion, and I was now in a situation which could not make any extraordinary exertions to disengage itself from either—I found myself with child.

" At last the wretch, who had thus trained me to destruction, hinted the purpose for which those means had been used. I discovered her to be an artful procuress for the pleasures of those who are men of decency to the world in the midst of debauchery.

" I roused every spark of courage within me at the horrid proposal. She treated my passion at first somewhat mildly, but when I continued to exert it she resented it with insult, and told me plainly that if I did not soon comply with her desires I should pay her every farthing I owed, or rot in a jail for life. I trembled at the thought; still, however, I resisted her importunities, and she put her threats in execution. I was conveyed to prison, weak from my condition, weaker from that struggle of grief and misery which for some time I had suffered. A miscarriage was the consequence.

" Amidst all the horrors of such a state, surrounded with wretches totally callous, lost alike to humanity and to shame, think, Mr. Harley, think what I endured; nor wonder that I at last yielded to the solicitations of that miscreant I had seen at her house, and sunk to the prostitution which he tempted. But that was happiness compared to what I have suffered since. He soon abandoned me to the common use of the town, and I was cast among those miserable beings in whose society I have since remained.

"Oh! did the daughters of virtue know our sufferings; did they see our hearts torn with anguish amidst the affectation of gaiety which our faces are obliged to assume! our bodies tortured by disease, our minds with that consciousness which they cannot lose! Did they know, did they think of this, Mr. Harley! Their censures are just, but their pity perhaps might spare the wretches whom their justice should condemn.

"Last night, but for an exertion of benevolence which the infection of our infamy prevents even in the humane, had I been thrust out from this miserable place which misfortune has yet left me; exposed to the brutal insults of drunkenness, or dragged by that justice which I could not bribe, to the punishment which may correct, but, alas! can never amend the abandoned objects of its terrors. From that, Mr. Harley, your goodness has relieved me."

He beckoned with his hand: he would have stopped the mention of his favours; but he could not speak, had it been to beg a diadem.

She saw his tears; her fortitude began to fail at the sight, when the voice of some stranger on the stairs awakened her attention. She listened for a moment, then starting up, exclaimed, "Merciful God! my father's voice!"

She had scarce uttered the word, when the door burst open, and a man entered in the garb of an officer. When he discovered his daughter and Harley, he started back a few paces; his look assumed a furious wildness! he laid his hand on his sword. The two objects of his wrath did not utter a syllable.

"Villain," he cried, "thou seest a father who had once a daughter's honour to preserve; blasted as it now is, behold him ready to avenge its loss!"

Harley had by this time some power of utterance. "Sir," said he, "if you will be a moment calm—"

"Infamous coward!" interrupted the other, "dost thou preach calmness to wrongs like mine?"

He drew his sword.

"Sir," said Harley, "let me tell you"—the blood ran quicker to his cheek, his pulse beat one, no more, and regained the temperament of humanity—"you are deceived, sir," said he, "you are much deceived; but I forgive suspicions which

45

your misfortunes have justified: I would not wrong you, upon my soul I would not, for the dearest gratification of a thousand worlds; my heart bleeds for you!"

His daughter was now prostrate at his feet. "Strike," said she, "strike here a wretch, whose misery cannot end but with that death she deserves."

Her hair had fallen on her shoulders! her look had the horrid calmness of out-breathed despair! Her father would have spoken; his lip quivered, his cheek grew pale, his eyes lost the lightning of their fury! there was a reproach in them, but with a mingling of pity. He turned them up to heaven, then on his daughter. He laid his left hand on his heart, the sword dropped from his right, he burst into tears.

———

CHAPTER XXIX

THE DISTRESSES OF A FATHER

HARLEY kneeled also at the side of the unfortunate daughter.

"Allow me, sir," said he, "to entreat your pardon for one whose offences have been already so signally punished. I know, I feel, that those tears, wrung from the heart of a father, are more dreadful to her than all the punishments your sword could have inflicted: accept the contrition of a child whom heaven has restored to you."

"Is she not lost," answered he, "irrecoverably lost? Damnation! a common prostitute to the meanest ruffian!"

"Calmly, my dear sir," said Harley, "did you know by what complicated misfortunes she has fallen to that miserable state in which you now behold her, I should have no need of words to excite your compassion. Think, sir, of what once she was. Would you abandon her to the insults of an unfeeling world, deny her opportunity of penitence, and cut off the little comfort that still remains for your afflictions and her own!"

"Speak," said he, addressing himself to his daughter; "speak; I will hear thee."

The desperation that supported her was lost; she fell to the ground, and bathed his feet with her tears.

Harley undertook her cause: he related the treacheries to which she had fallen a sacrifice, and again solicited the forgiveness of her father. He looked on her for some time in silence; the pride of a soldier's honour checked for a while the yearnings of his heart; but nature at last prevailed, he fell on her neck and mingled his tears with hers.

Harley, who discovered from the dress of the stranger that he was just arrived from a journey, begged that they would both remove to his lodgings, till he could procure others for them. Atkins looked at him with some marks of surprise. His daughter now first recovered the power of speech.

"Wretch as I am," said she, "yet there is some gratitude due to the preserver of your child. See him now before you. To him I owe my life, or at least the comfort of imploring your forgiveness before I die."

"Pardon me, young gentleman," said Atkins, "I fear my passion wronged you."

"Never, never, sir," said Harley; "if it had, your reconciliation to your daughter were an atonement a thousand fold." He then repeated his request that he might be allowed to conduct them to his lodgings, to which Mr. Atkins at last consented. He took his daughter's arm.

"Come, my Emily," said he, "we can never, never recover that happiness we have lost! but time may teach us to remember our misfortunes with patience."

When they arrived at the house where Harley lodged, he was informed that the first floor was then vacant, and that the gentleman and his daughter might be accommodated there. While he was upon his enquiry, Miss Atkins informed her father more particularly what she owed to his benevolence. When he returned into the room where they were Atkins ran and embraced him; begged him again to forgive the offence he had given him, and made the warmest protestations of gratitude for his favours. We would attempt to describe the joy which Harley felt on this occasion, did it not occur to us that one half of the world could not understand it though we did, and the other half will, by this time, have understood it without any description at all.

Miss Atkins now retired to her chamber, to take some rest from the violence of the emotions she had suffered. When she was gone, her father, addressing himself to Harley, said, " You have a right, sir, to be informed of the present situation of one who owes so much to your compassion for his misfortunes. My daughter I find has informed you what that was at the fatal juncture when they began. Her distresses you have heard, you have pitied as they deserved; with mine, perhaps, I cannot so easily make you acquainted. You have a feeling heart, Mr. Harley; I bless it that it has saved my child; but you never were a father, a father torn by that most dreadful of calamities, the dishonour of a child he doated on! You have been already informed of some of the circumstances of her elopement. I was then from home, called by the death of a relation, who, though he would never advance me a shilling on the utmost exigency in his life-time, left me all the gleanings of his frugality at his death. I would not write this intelligence to my daughter, because I intended to be the bearer myself; and as soon as my business would allow me, I set out on my return, winged with all the haste of paternal affection. I fondly built those schemes of future happiness, which present prosperity is ever busy to suggest: my Emily was concerned in them all. As I approached our little dwelling my heart throbbed with the anticipation of joy and welcome. I imagined the cheering fire, the blissful contentment of a frugal meal, made luxurious by a daughter's smile, I painted to myself her surprise at the tidings of our new-acquired riches, our fond disputes about the disposal of them.

" The road was shortened by the dreams of happiness I enjoyed, and it began to be dark as I reached the house: I alighted from my horse, and walked softly upstairs to the room we commonly sat in. I was somewhat disappointed at not finding my daughter there. I rung the bell; her maid appeared, and shewed no small signs of wonder at the summons. She blessed herself as she entered the room: I smiled at her surprise. ' Where is Miss Emily, sir?' said she.

" ' Emily!'

" ' Yes, sir; she has been gone hence some days, upon receipt of those letters you sent her.'

" ' Letters!' said I.

48

" ' Yes, sir, so she told me, and went off in all haste that very night.'

" I stood aghast as she spoke, but was able so far to recollect myself, as to put on the affectation of calmness, and telling her there was certainly some mistake in the affair, desired her to leave me.

" When she was gone, I threw myself into a chair, in that state of uncertainty which is, of all others, the most dreadful. The gay visions with which I had delighted myself, vanished in an instant. I was tortured with tracing back the same circle of doubt and disappointment. My head grew dizzy as I thought. I called the servant again, and asked her a hundred questions, to no purpose; there was not room even for conjecture.

" Something at last arose in my mind, which we call Hope, without knowing what it is. I wished myself deluded by it; but it could not prevail over my returning fears. I arose and walked through the room. My Emily's spinnet stood at the end of it, open, with a book of music folded down at some of my favourite lessons. I touched the keys; there was a vibration in the sound that froze my blood; I looked around, and methought the family pictures on the walls gazed on me with compassion in their faces. I sat down again with an attempt at more composure; I started at every creaking of the door, and my ears rung with imaginary noises!

" I had not remained long in this situation, when the arrival of a friend, who had accidentally heard of my return, put an end to my doubts, by the recital of my daughter's dishonour. He told me he had his information from a young gentleman, to whom Winbrooke had boasted of having seduced her.

" I started from my seat, with broken curses on my lips, and without knowing whither I should pursue them, ordered my servant to load my pistols and saddle my horses. My friend, however, with great difficulty, persuaded me to compose myself for that night, promising to accompany me on the morrow, to Sir George Winbrooke's in quest of his son.

" The morrow came, after a night spent in a state little distant from madness. We went as early as decency would allow to Sir George's. He received me with politeness, and indeed compassion, protested his abhorrence of his son's conduct, and told me that he had set out some days before for London, on which place he had procured a draft for a large sum, on pretence of finishing his travels, but that he had not heard from him since his departure.

" I did not wait for any more, either of information or comfort, but, against the united remonstrances of Sir George and my friend, set out instantly for London, with a frantic uncertainty of purpose; but there, all manner of search was in vain. I could trace neither of them any farther than the inn where they first put up on their arrival; and after some days' fruitless inquiry, returned home destitute of every little hope that had hitherto supported me. The journeys I had made, the restless nights I had spent, above all, the perturbation of my mind, had the effect which naturally might be expected— a very dangerous fever was the consequence. From this, however, contrary to the expectation of my physicians, I recovered. It was now that I first felt something like calmness of mind; probably from being reduced to a state which could not produce the exertions of anguish or despair. A stupid melancholy settled on my soul; I could endure to live with an apathy of life; at times I forgot my resentment, and wept at the remembrance of my child.

" Such has been the tenor of my days since that fatal moment when these misfortunes began, till yesterday, that I received a letter from a friend in town, acquainting me of her present situation. Could such tales as mine, Mr. Harley, be sometimes suggested to the daughters of levity, did they but know with what anxiety the heart of a parent flutters round the child he loves, they would be less apt to construe into harshness that delicate concern for their conduct, which they often complain of as laying restraint upon things, to the young, the gay, and the thoughtless, seemingly harmless and indifferent. Alas! I fondly imagined that I needed not even these common cautions! my Emily was the joy of my age, and the pride of my soul! Those things are now no more, they are lost for ever! Her death I could have borne, but the death of her honour has added obloquy and shame to that sorrow which bends my grey hairs to the dust!"

As he spoke these last words, his voice trembled in his throat; it was now lost in his tears. He sat with his face half turned from Harley, as if he would have hid the sorrow which he felt. Harley was in the same attitude himself; he durst not meet Atkins' eye with a tear, but gathering his stifled breath, "Let me entreat you, sir," said he, "to hope better things. The world is ever tyrannical; it warps our sorrows to edge them with keener affliction. Let us not be slaves to the names it affixes to motive or to action. I know an ingenuous mind cannot help feeling when they sting. But there are considerations by which it may be overcome. Its fantastic ideas vanish as they rise; they teach us to look beyond it."

*   *   *   *   *   *

———

A FRAGMENT

SHOWING HIS SUCCESS WITH THE BARONET

* * THE card he received was in the politest style in which disappointment could be communicated. The baronet " was under a necessity of giving up his application for Mr. Harley, as he was informed that the lease was engaged for a gentleman who had long served His Majesty in another capacity, and whose merit had entitled him to the first lucrative thing that should be vacant." Even Harley could not murmur at such a disposal. " Perhaps," said he to himself, " some war-worn officer, who, like poor Atkins, had been neglected from reasons which merited the highest advancement; whose honour could not stoop to solicit the preferment he deserved; perhaps, with a family, taught the principles of delicacy, without the means of supporting it; a wife and children—gracious heaven! whom my wishes would have deprived of bread!——"

He was interrupted in his reverie by some one tapping him on the shoulder, and, on turning round, he discovered it to be the very man who had explained to him the condition of his gay companion at Hyde Park Corner. " I am glad to see you, sir," said he; " I believe we are fellows in disappointment." Harley started, and said that he was at a loss to understand him. "Pooh! you need not be so shy," answered the other; "every one for himself is but fair, and I had much rather you had got it than the rascally gauger." Harley still protested his ignorance of what he meant. "Why, the lease of Bancroft Manor; had not you been applying for it?" "I confess I was," replied Harley; "but I cannot conceive how you should be interested in the matter." "Why, I was making interest for it myself," said he, "and I think I had some title. I voted for this same baronet at the last election, and made some of my friends do so too; though I would not have you imagine that I sold my vote. No, I scorn it, let me tell you I scorn it; but I thought as how this man was staunch and true, and I find he's but a double-faced fellow after all, and speechifies in the House for any side he hopes to make most by. Oh, how many fine speeches and squeezings by the hand we had of him on the canvass! 'And if ever I shall be so happy as to have an opportunity of serving you.' A murrain on the smooth-tongued knave, and after all to get it for this pimp of a gauger." "The gauger! there must be some mistake," said Harley. "He writes me, that it was engaged for one whose long services——" "Services!" interrupted the other; "you shall hear. Services! Yes, his sister arrived in town a few days ago, and is now sempstress to the baronet. A plague on all rogues, says honest Sam Wrightson. I shall but just drink damnation to them to-night, in a crown's worth of Ashley's, and leave London to-morrow by sun-rise." "I shall leave it too," said Harley; and so he accordingly did.

In passing through Piccadilly, he had observed, on the window of an inn, a notification of the departure of a stage-coach for a place in his road homewards; in the way back to his lodgings, he took a seat in it for his return.

———

CHAPTER XXXIII

HE LEAVES LONDON—CHARACTERS IN A STAGE-COACH

THE company in the stage-coach consisted of a grocer and his wife, who were going to pay a visit to some of their country friends; a young officer, who took this way of marching to quarters; a middle-aged gentlewoman, who had been hired as housekeeper to some family in the country; and an elderly, well-looking man, with a remarkable old-fashioned periwig.

Harley, upon entering, discovered but one vacant seat, next the grocer's wife, which, from his natural shyness of temper, he made no scruple to occupy, however aware that being driven backwards always disagreed with him.

Though his inclination to physiognomy had met with some rubs in the metropolis, he had not yet lost his attachment to that science. He set himself, therefore, to examine, as usual, the countenances of his companions. Here, indeed, he was not long in doubt as to the preference; for besides that the elderly gentleman, who sat opposite to him, had features by nature more expressive of good dispositions, there was something in that periwig we mentioned, peculiarly attractive of Harley's regard.

He had not been long employed in these speculations, when he found himself attacked with that faintish sickness, which was the natural consequence of his situation in the coach. The paleness of his countenance was first observed by the housekeeper, who immediately made offer of her smelling bottle, which Harley, however, declined, telling at the same time the cause of his uneasiness. The gentleman, on the opposite side of the coach, now first turned his eye from the side direction in which it had been fixed, and begged Harley to exchange places with him, expressing his regret that he had not made the proposal before. Harley thanked him, and, upon being assured that both seats were alike to him, was about to accept of his offer, when the young gentleman of the sword, putting on an arch look, laid hold of the other's arm. " So, my old boy," said he, " I find you have still some youthful blood about you, but, with your leave, I will do myself the honour of sitting by this lady;" and took his place accordingly. The grocer stared him as full in the face as his own short neck would allow, and his wife, who was a little, round-faced woman, with a great deal of colour in her cheeks, drew up at the compliment that was paid her, looking first at the officer, and then at the housekeeper.

This incident was productive of some discourse; for before, though there was sometimes a cough or a hem from the grocer, and the officer now and then humm'd a few notes of a song, there had not a single word passed the lips of any of the company.

Mrs. Grocer observed, how ill-convenient it was for people, who could not bear to ride backwards, to travel in a stage. This brought on a dissertation on stage-coaches in general, and the pleasure of keeping a chay of one's own; which led to another, on the great riches of Mr. Deputy Bearskin, who, according to her, had once been of that industrious order of youths who sweep the crossings of the streets for the conveniency of passengers, but, by various fortunate accidents, had now acquired an immense fortune, and kept his coach and a dozen livery servants. All this afforded ample fund for conversation, if conversation it might be called, that was carried on solely by the before-mentioned lady, nobody offering to interrupt her, except that the officer sometimes signified his approbation by a variety of oaths, a sort of phraseology in which he seemed extremely conversant. She appealed indeed, frequently, to her husband for the authenticity of certain facts, of which the good man as often protested his total ignorance; but as he was always called fool, or something very like it, for his pains, he at last contrived to support the credit of his wife without prejudice to his conscience, and signified his assent by a noise not unlike the grunting of that animal which in shape and fatness he somewhat resembled.

The housekeeper, and the old gentleman who sat next to Harley, were now observed to be fast asleep, at which the lady, who had been at such pains to entertain them, muttered some words of displeasure, and, upon the officer's whispering to smoke the old put, both she and her husband pursed up their mouths into a contemptuous smile. Harley looked sternly on the grocer. "You are come, sir," said he, "to those years when you might have learned some reverence for age. As for this young man, who has so lately escaped from the nursery, he may be allowed to divert himself." "Damme, sir!" said the officer, "do you call me young?" striking up the front of his hat, and stretching forward on his seat, till his face almost touched Harley's. It is probable, however, that he discovered something there which tended to pacify him, for, on the ladies entreating them not to quarrel, he very soon resumed his posture and calmness together, and was rather less profuse of his oaths during the rest of the journey.

It is possible the old gentleman had waked time enough to hear the last part of this discourse; at least (whether from that cause, or that he too was a physiognomist) he wore a look remarkably complacent to Harley, who, on his part, shewed a particular observance of him. Indeed, they had soon a better opportunity of making their acquaintance, as the coach arrived that night at the town where the officer's regiment lay, and the places of destination of their other fellow-travellers, it seems, were at no great distance, for, next morning, the old gentleman and Harley were the only passengers remaining.

When they left the inn in the morning, Harley, pulling out a little pocket-book, began to examine the contents, and make some corrections with a pencil. " This," said he, turning to his companion, " is an amusement with which I sometimes pass idle hours at an inn. These are quotations from those humble poets, who trust their fame to the brittle tenure of windows and drinking-glasses." " From our inns," returned the gentleman, " a stranger might imagine that we were a nation of poets; machines, at least, containing poetry, which the motion of a journey emptied of their contents. Is it from the vanity of being thought geniuses, or a mere mechanical imitation of the custom of others, that we are tempted to scrawl rhyme upon such places? "

" Whether vanity is the cause of our becoming rhymesters or not," answered Harley, " it is a pretty certain effect of it. An old man of my acquaintance, who dealt in apothegms, used to say that he had known few men without envy, few wits without ill-nature, and no poet without vanity; and I believe his remark is a pretty just one. Vanity has been immemorially the charter of poets. In this, the ancients were more honest than we are. The old poets frequently make boastful predictions of the immortality their works will obtain for them; ours, in their dedications and prefatory discourses, employ much eloquence to praise their patrons, and much seeming honesty to condemn themselves, or at least to apologise for their productions to the world. But this, in my opinion, is the more assuming manner of the two; for of all the garbs I ever saw Pride put on, that of her humility is to me the most disgusting."

"It is natural enough for a poet to be vain," said the stranger. "The little worlds which he raises, the inspiration which he claims, may easily be productive of self-importance; though that inspiration is fabulous, it brings on egotism, which is always the parent of vanity."

"It may be supposed," answered Harley, "that inspiration of old was an article of religious faith; in modern times it may be translated a propensity to compose; and I believe it is not always most readily found where the poets have fixed its residence, amidst groves and plains, and the scenes of pastoral retirement. The mind may be there unbent from the cares of the world, but it will frequently, at the same time, be unnerved from any great exertion. It will feel the languor of·indolence, and wander without effort over the regions of reflection.

"There is at least," said the stranger, "one advantage in the poetical inclination, that it is an incentive to philanthropy. There is a certain poetic ground, on which a man cannot tread without feelings that enlarge the heart: the causes of human depravity vanish before the romantic enthusiasm he professes, and many who are not able to reach the Parnassian heights, may yet approach so near as to be bettered by the air of the climate."

"I have always thought so," replied Harley; "but this is an argument with the prudent against it: they urge the danger of unfitness for the world."

"I allow it," returned the other; "but I believe it is not always rightfully imputed to the bent for poetry: that is only one effect of the common cause.—Jack, says his father, is indeed no scholar; nor could all the drubbings from his master ever bring him one step forward in his accidence or syntax: but I intend him for a merchant.—Allow the same indulgence to Tom.—Tom reads Virgil and Horace when he should be casting accounts; and but t'other day he pawned his great-coat for an edition of Shakespeare.—But Tom would have been as he is, though Virgil and Horace had never been born, though Shakespeare had died a link-boy; for his nurse will tell you, that when he was a child, he broke his rattle, to discover what it was that sounded within it; and burnt the sticks of his go-cart, because he liked to see the sparkling of timber in the fire.—'Tis a sad case; but what is to be done?— Why, Jack shall make a fortune, dine on venison, and drink claret.—Ay, but Tom—Tom shall dine with his brother, when his pride will let him; at other times, he shall bless God over a half-pint of ale and a Welsh-rabbit; and both shall go to heaven as they may.—That's a poor prospect for Tom, says the father.—To go to heaven! I cannot agree with him."

"Perhaps," said Harley, "we now-a-days discourage the romantic turn a little too much. Our boys are prudent too soon. Mistake me not, I do not mean to blame them for want of levity or dissipation; but their pleasures are those of hackneyed vice, blunted to every finer emotion by the repetition of debauch; and their desire of pleasure is warped to the desire of wealth, as the means of procuring it. The immense riches acquired by individuals have erected a standard of ambition, destructive of private morals, and of public virtue. The weaknesses of vice are left us; but the most allowable of our failings we are taught to despise. Love, the passion most natural to the sensibility of youth, has lost the plaintive dignity it once possessed, for the unmeaning simper of a dangling coxcomb; and the only serious concern, that of a dowry, is settled, even amongst the beardless leaders of the dancing-school. The Frivolous and the Interested (might a satirist say) are the characteristical features of the age; they are visible even in the essays of our philosophers. They laugh at the pedantry of our fathers, who complained of the times in which they lived; they are at pains to persuade us how much those were deceived; they pride themselves in defending things as they find them, and in exploding the barren sounds which had been reared into motives for action. To this their style is suited; and the manly tone of reason is exchanged for perpetual efforts at sneer and ridicule. This I hold to be an alarming crisis in the corruption of a state; when not only is virtue declined, and vice prevailing, but when the praises of virtue are forgotten, and the infamy of vice unfelt."

They soon after arrived at the next inn upon the route of the stage-coach, when the stranger told Harley, that his brother's house, to which he was returning, lay at no great distance, and he must therefore unwillingly bid him adieu.

"I should like," said Harley, taking his hand, "to have some word to remember so much seeming worth by: my name is Harley."

"I shall remember it," answered the old gentleman, "in my prayers; mine is Silton."

And Silton indeed it was! Ben Silton himself! Once more, my honoured friend, farewell!——Born to be happy without the world, to that peaceful happiness which the world has not to bestow! Envy never scowled on thy life, nor hatred smiled on thy grave.

———

CHAPTER XXXIV

HE MEETS AN OLD ACQUAINTANCE

WHEN the stage-coach arrived at the place of its destination, Harley began to consider how he should proceed the remaining part of his journey. He was very civilly accosted by the master of the inn, who offered to accommodate him either with a post-chaise or horses, to any distance he had a mind: but as he did things frequently in a way different from what other people call natural, he refused these offers, and set out immediately a-foot, having first put a spare shirt in his pocket, and given directions for the forwarding of his portmanteau. This was a method of travelling which he was accustomed to take: it saved the trouble of provision for any animal but himself, and left him at liberty to choose his quarters, either at an inn, or at the first cottage in which he saw a face he liked: nay, when he was not peculiarly attracted by the reasonable creation, he would sometimes consort with a species of inferior rank, and lay himself down to sleep by the side of a rock, or on the banks of a rivulet. He did few things without a motive, but his motives were rather eccentric: and the usual and expedient were terms which he held to be very indefinite, and which therefore he did not always apply to the sense in which they are commonly understood.

The sun was now in his decline, and the evening remarkably

serene, when he entered a hollow part of the road, which
winded between the surrounding banks, and seamed the sward
in different lines, as the choice of travellers had directed them
to tread it. It seemed to be little frequented now, for some
of those had partly recovered their former verdure. The
scene was such as induced Harley to stand and enjoy it; when,
turning round, his notice was attracted by an object, which
the fixture of his eye on the spot he walked had before prevented him from observing.

An old man, who from his dress seemed to have been a
soldier, lay fast asleep on the ground; a knapsack rested on
a stone at his right hand, while his staff and brass-hilted
sword were crossed at his left.

Harley looked on him with the most earnest attention. He
was one of those figures which Salvator would have drawn;
nor was the surrounding scenery unlike the wildness of that
painter's back-grounds. The banks on each side were covered
with fantastic shrub-wood, and at a little distance, on the top
of one of them, stood a finger-post, to mark the directions of
two roads which diverged from the point where it was placed.
A rock, with some dangling wild flowers, jutted out above
where the soldier lay; on which grew the stump of a large
tree, white with age, and a single twisted branch shaded his
face as he slept. His face had the marks of manly comeliness
impaired by time; his forehead was not altogether bald, but
its hairs might have been numbered; while a few white locks
behind crossed the brown of his neck with a contrast the most
venerable to a mind like Harley's. "Thou art old," said he
to himself; "but age has not brought thee rest for its infirmities; I fear those silver hairs have not found shelter from thy
country, though that neck has been bronzed in its service."
The stranger waked. He looked at Harley with the appearance of some confusion: it was a pain the latter knew too well
to think of causing in another; he turned and went on. The
old man re-adjusted his knapsack, and followed in one of the
tracks on the opposite side of the road.

When Harley heard the tread of his feet behind him, he
could not help stealing back a glance at his fellow-traveller.
He seemed to bend under the weight of his knapsack; he
halted in his walk, and one of his arms was supported by a

sling, and lay motionless across his breast. He had that steady look of sorrow, which indicates that its owner has gazed upon his griefs till he has forgotten to lament them; yet not without those streaks of complacency which a good mind will sometimes throw into the countenance, through all the incumbent load of its depression.

He had now advanced nearer to Harley, and, with an uncertain sort of voice, begged to know what it was o'clock; " I fear," said he, " sleep has beguiled me of my time, and I shall hardly have light enough left to carry me to the end of my journey."

" Father!" said Harley (who by this time found the romantic enthusiasm rising within him) " how far do you mean to go?"

" But a little way, sir," returned the other; " and indeed it is but a little way I can manage now: 'tis just four miles from the height to the village, whither I am going."

" I am going thither too," said Harley; " we may make the road shorter to each other. You seem to have served your country, sir, to have served it hardly too; 'tis a character I have the highest esteem for.—I would not be impertinently inquisitive; but there is that in your appearance which excites my curiosity to know something more of you; in the meantime, suffer me to carry that knapsack."

The old man gazed on him; a tear stood in his eye! " Young gentleman," said he, " you are too good; may Heaven bless you for an old man's sake, who has nothing but his blessing to give! but my knapsack is so familiar to my shoulders, that I should walk the worse for wanting it; and it would be troublesome to you, who have not been used to its weight."

" Far from it," answered Harley, " I should tread the lighter; it would be the most honourable badge I ever wore."

" Sir," said the stranger, who had looked earnestly in Harley's face during the last part of his discourse, " is not your name Harley?"

" It is," replied he; " I am ashamed to say I have forgotten yours."

" You may well have forgotten my face," said the stranger; —'tis a long time since you saw it; but possibly you may remember something of old Edwards."

" Edwards!" cried Harley, " oh! heavens?" and sprung
to embrace him; " let me clasp those knees on which I have sat
so often: Edwards!—I shall never forget that fire-side, round
which I have been so happy! But where, where have you
been? where is Jack? where is your daughter? How has it
fared with them, when fortune, I fear, has been so unkind
to you?"

" 'Tis a long tale," replied Edwards; " but I will try to tell
it you as we walk.

" When you were at school in the neighbourhood, you remember me at South-hill: that farm had been possessed by my
father, grandfather, and great-grandfather, which last was a
younger brother of that very man's ancestor, who is now lord
of the manor. I thought I managed it, as they had done, with
prudence; I paid my rent regularly as it became due, and had
always as much behind as gave bread to me and my children.
But my last lease was out soon after you left that part of the
country; and the squire, who had lately got a London-attorney
for his steward, would not renew it, because, he said, he did
not choose to have any farm under £300 a year value on his
estate; but offered to give me the preference on the same terms
with another, if I chose to take the one he had marked out, of
which mine was a part.

" What could I do, Mr. Harley? I feared the undertaking
was too great for me; yet to leave, at my age, the house I had
lived in from my cradle! I could not, Mr. Harley, I could
not; there was not a tree about it that I did not look on as
my father, my brother, or my child: so I even ran the risk,
and took the squire's offer of the whole. But I had soon reason to repent of my bargain; the steward had taken care that
my former farm should be the best land of the division: I was
obliged to hire more servants, and I could not have my eye
over them all; some unfavourable seasons followed one another, and I found my affairs entangling on my hands. To
add to my distress, a considerable corn-factor turned bankrupt
with a sum of mine in his possession: I failed paying my
rent so punctually as I was wont to do, and the same steward
had my stock taken in execution in a few days after. So, Mr.
Harley, there was an end of my prosperity. However, there
was as much produced from the sale of my effects as paid

my debts and saved me from a jail: I thank God I wronged
no man, and the world could never charge me with dishonesty.

"Had you seen us, Mr. Harley, when we were turned out
of South-hill, I am sure you would have wept at the sight.
You remember old Trusty, my shag house-dog; I shall never
forget it while I live; the poor creature was blind with age,
and could scarce crawl after us to the door; he went however
as far as the gooseberry-bush; which you may remember stood
on the left side of the yard; he was wont to bask in the sun
there; when he had reached that spot, he stopped; we went
on: I called to him; he wagged his tail, but did not stir: I
called again; he lay down: I whistled, and cried Trusty; he
gave a short howl, and died! I could have lain down and
died too; but God gave me strength to live for my children."

The old man now paused a moment to take breath. He
eyed Harley's face; it was bathed with tears: the story was
grown familiar to himself; he dropped one tear, and no more.

"Though I was poor," continued he, "I was not altogether
without credit. A gentleman in the neighbourhood, who had
a small farm unoccupied at the time, offered to let me have it,
on giving security for the rent; which I made shift to procure.
It was a piece of ground which required management to make
anything of; but it was nearly within the compass of my son's
labour and my own. We exerted all our industry to bring it
into some heart. We began to succeed tolerably, and lived
contented on its produce, when an unlucky accident brought
'us under the displeasure of a neighbouring justice of the
peace, and broke all our family happiness again.

"My son was a remarkable good shooter; he had always
kept a pointer on our former farm, and thought no harm in
doing so now; when one day, having sprung a covey of partridges in our own ground, the dog, of his own accord, followed
them into the justice's. My son laid down his gun, and went
after his dog to bring him back: the game-keeper, who had
marked the birds, came up, and seeing the pointer, shot him
just as my son approached. The creature fell; my son ran up
to him: he died with a complaining sort of cry at his master's
feet. Jack could bear it no longer; but, flying at the game-
keeper, wrenched his gun out of his hand, and with the butt
end of it, felled him to the ground.

THE MAN OF FEELING

" He had scarce got home, when a constable came with a warrant, and dragged him to prison; there he lay, for the justices would not take bail, till he was tried at the quarter-sessions for the assault and battery. His fine was hard upon us to pay; we contrived however to live the worse for it, and make up the loss by our frugality: but the justice was not content with that punishment, and soon after had an opportunity of punishing us indeed.

" An officer with press-orders came down to our country, and having met with the justices, agreed that they should pitch on a certain number, who could most easily be spared from the county, of whom he would take care to clear it: my son's name was in the justices' list.

" 'Twas on a Christmas eve, and the birth-day too of my son's little boy. The night was piercing cold, and it blew a storm, with showers of hail and snow. We had made up a cheering fire in an inner room; I sat before it in my wicker-chair, blessing providence, that had still left a shelter for me and my children. My son's two little ones were holding their gambols around us; my heart warmed at the sight: I brought a bottle of my best ale, and all our misfortunes were forgotten.

" It had long been our custom to play a game at blind man's buff on that night, and it was not omitted now; so to it we fell, I, and my son, and his wife, the daughter of a neighbouring farmer, who happened to be with us at the time, the two children, and an old maid servant, who had lived with me from a child. The lot fell on my son to be blindfolded: we had continued some time at our game, when he groped his way into an outer room in pursuit of some of us, who, he imagined, had taken shelter there; we kept snug in our places, and enjoyed his mistake. He had not been long there, when he was suddenly seized from behind; ' I shall have you now,' said he, and turned about. ' Shall you so, master?' answered the ruffian, who had laid hold of him; ' we shall make you play at another sort of game by and by.' "—At these words Harley started with a convulsive sort of motion, and grasping Edwards's sword, drew it half out of the scabbard, with a look of the most frantic wildness. Edwards gently replaced it in its sheath, and went on with his relation.

" On hearing these words in a strange voice, we all rushed

out to discover the cause; the room by this time was almost full of the gang. My daughter-in-law fainted at the sight; the maid and I ran to assist her, while my poor son remained motionless, gazing by turns on his children and their mother. We soon recovered her to life, and begged her to retire and wait the issue of the affair; but she flew to her husband, and clung round him in an agony of terror and grief.

"In the gang was one of a smoother aspect, whom, by his dress, we discovered to be a serjeant of foot: he came up to me, and told me, that my son had his choice of the sea or land service, whispering at the same time that, if he chose the land, he might get off, on procuring him another man, and paying a certain sum for his freedom. The money we could just muster up in the house, by the assistance of the maid, who produced, in a green bag, all the little savings of her service; but the man we could not expect to find. My daughter-in-law gazed upon her children with a look of the wildest despair: 'My poor infants!' said she, 'your father is forced from you; who shall now labour for your bread? or must your mother beg for herself and you?' I prayed her to be patient; but comfort I had none to give her. At last, calling the serjeant aside, I asked him, 'If I was too old to be accepted in place of my son?'

"'Why, I don't know,' said he; 'you are rather old to be sure, but yet the money may do much.'

"I put the money in his hand, and coming back to my children, 'Jack,' said I, 'you are free; live to give your wife and these little ones bread; I will go, my child, in your stead; I have but little life to lose, and if I staid, I should add one to the wretches you left behind.'

"'No,' replied my son, 'I am not that coward you imagine me; heaven forbid that my father's grey hairs should be so exposed, while I sat idle at home; I am young and able to endure much, and God will take care of you and my family.'

"'Jack,' said I, 'I will put an end to this matter, you have never hitherto disobeyed me; I will not be contradicted in this; stay at home, I charge you, and, for my sake, be kind to my children.'

"Our parting, Mr. Harley, I cannot describe to you; it was the first time we ever had parted: the very press-gang could scarce keep from tears; but the serjeant, who had seemed the softest before, was now the least moved of them all. He conducted me to a party of new-raised recruits, who lay at a village in the neighbourhood; and we soon after joined the regiment. I had not been long with it when we were ordered to the East Indies, where I was soon made a serjeant, and might have picked up some money, if my heart had been as hard as some others were; but my nature was never of that kind, that could think of getting rich at the expense of my conscience.

" Amongst our prisoners was an old Indian, whom some of our officers supposed to have a treasure hidden somewhere; which is no uncommon practice in that country. They pressed him to discover it. He declared he had none, but that would not satisfy them, so they ordered him to be tied to a stake, and suffer fifty lashes every morning till he should learn to speak out, as they said. Oh! Mr. Harley, had you seen him, as I did, with his hands bound behind him, suffering in silence, while the big drops trickled down his shrivelled cheeks and wet his grey beard, which some of the inhuman soldiers plucked in scorn! I could not bear it, I could not for my soul, and one morning, when the rest of the guard were out of the way, I found means to let him escape. I was tried by a court-martial for negligence on my post, and ordered, in compassion of my age, and having got this wound in my arm and that in my leg in the service, only to suffer three hundred lashes and be turned out of the regiment; but my sentence was mitigated as to the lashes, and I had only two hundred. When I had suffered these I was turned out of the camp, and had betwixt three and four hundred miles to travel before I could reach a sea-port, without guide to conduct me, or money to buy me provisions by the way. I set out, however, resolved to walk as far as I could, and then to lay myself down and die. But I had scarce gone a mile when I was met by the Indian whom I had delivered. He pressed me in his arms, and kissed the marks of the lashes on my back a thousand times; he led me to a little hut, where some friend of his dwelt, and after I was recovered of my wounds conducted me so far on my journey himself, and sent another Indian to guide me through the rest. When we parted he pulled out a purse with two hundred pieces of gold in it. 'Take this,' said he, 'my dear preserver, it is all I have been able to procure.'

"I begged him not to bring himself to poverty for my sake, who should probably have no need of it long, but he insisted on my accepting it. He embraced me. 'You are an Englishman,' said he, 'but the Great Spirit has given you an Indian heart, may He bear up the weight of your old age, and blunt the arrow that brings it rest!'

"We parted, and not long after I made shift to get my passage to England. 'Tis but about a week since I landed, and I am going to end my days in the arms of my son. This sum may be of use to him and his children, 'tis all the value I put upon it. I thank Heaven I never was covetous of wealth; I never had much, but was always so happy as to be content with my little."

When Edwards had ended his relation, Harley stood a while looking at him in silence; at last he pressed him in his arms, and when he had given vent to the fulness of his heart by a shower of tears, "Edwards," said he, "let me hold thee to my bosom, let me imprint the virtue of thy sufferings on my soul. Come, my honoured veteran! let me endeavour to soften the last days of a life, worn out in the service of humanity; call me also thy son, and let me cherish thee as a father."

Edwards, from whom the recollection of his own sufferings had scarce forced a tear, now blubbered like a boy: he could not speak his gratitude, but by some short exclamations of blessings upon Harley.

CHAPTER XXXV

HE MISSES AN OLD ACQUAINTANCE.—AN ADVENTURE CONSEQUENT UPON IT

WHEN they had arrived within a little way of the village they journeyed to, Harley stopped short, and looked steadfastly on the mouldering walls of a ruined house that stood on the road side. "Oh, heavens!" he cried, "what do I see: silent, unroofed, and desolate! Are all the gay tenants gone? do I hear their hum no more? Edwards, look there, look there! the scene of my infant joys, my earliest friendships, laid waste and ruinous! That was the very school where I was boarded when you were at South-hill; 'tis but a twelve-month since I saw it standing, and its benches filled with little cherubs: that opposite side of the road was the green on which they sported; see it now ploughed up! I would have given fifty times its value to have saved it from the sacrilege of that plough."

"Dear sir," replied Edwards, "perhaps they have left it from choice, and may have got another spot as good."

"They cannot," said Harley, "they cannot; I shall never see the sward covered with its daisies, nor pressed by the dance of the dear innocents: I shall never see that stump decked with the garlands which their little hands had gathered. These two long stones, which now lie at the foot of it, were once the supports of a hut I myself assisted to rear: I have sat on the sods within it, when we had spread our banquet of apples before us, and been more blessed—Oh! Edwards, infinitely more blessed, than ever I shall be again."

Just then a woman passed them on the road, and discovered some signs of wonder at the attitude of Harley, who stood, with his hands folded together, looking with a moistened eye on the fallen pillars of the hut. He was too much entranced in thought to observe her at all, but Edwards, civilly accosting her, desired to know if that had not been the school-house, and how it came into the condition in which they now saw it.

"Alack a day!" said she, "it was the school-house indeed; but to be sure, sir, the squire has pulled it down because it stood in the way of his prospects."

"What! how! prospects! pulled down!" cried Harley.

"Yes, to be sure, sir; and the green, where the children used to play, he has ploughed up, because, he said, they hurt his fence on the other side of it."

"Curses on his narrow heart," cried Harley, "that could violate a right so sacred! Heaven blast the wretch!

"And from his derogate body never spring
A babe to honour him!"——

But I need not, Edwards, I need not" (recovering himself a little), "he is cursed enough already: to him the noblest source of happiness is denied, and the cares of his sordid soul shall gnaw it, while thou sittest over a brown crust, smiling on those mangled limbs that have saved thy son and his children!"

"If you want anything with the school-mistress, sir," said the woman, "I can show you the way to her house."

He followed her without knowing whither he went.

They stopped at the door of a snug habitation, where sat an elderly woman with a boy and a girl before her, each of whom held a supper of bread and milk in their hands.

"There, sir, is the school-mistress."

"Madam," said Harley, "was not an old venerable man school-master here some time ago?"

"Yes, sir, he was, poor man; the loss of his former school-house, I believe, broke his heart, for he died soon after it was taken down, and as another has not yet been found, I have that charge in the meantime."

"And this boy and girl, I presume, are your pupils?"

"Ay, sir; they are poor orphans, put under my care by the parish, and more promising children I never saw."

"Orphans?" said Harley.

"Yes, sir, of honest creditable parents as any in the parish, and it is a shame for some folks to forget their relations at a time when they have most need to remember them."

"Madam," said Harley, "let us never forget that we are all relations."

He kissed the children.

"Their father, sir," continued she, "was a farmer here in the neighbourhood, and a sober industrious man he was; but nobody can help misfortunes: what with bad crops, and bad debts, which are worse, his affairs went to wreck, and both he and his wife died of broken hearts. And a sweet couple they were, sir; there was not a properer man to look on in the county than John Edwards, and so indeed were all the Edwardses."

"What Edwardses?" cried the old soldier hastily.

"The Edwardses of South-hill, and a worthy family they were."

"South-hill!" said he, in a languid voice, and fell back into the arms of the astonished Harley. The school-mistress ran for some water and a smelling-bottle, with the assistance of which they soon recovered the unfortunate Edwards. He stared wildly for some time, then folding his orphan grand-children in his arms,

"Oh! my children, my children," he cried, "have I found you thus? My poor Jack, art thou gone? I thought thou shouldst have carried thy father's grey hairs to the grave! and these little ones"—his tears choked his utterance, and he fell again on the necks of the children.

"My dear old man," said Harley, "Providence has sent you to relieve them; it will bless me if I can be the means of assisting you."

"Yes, indeed, sir," answered the boy; "father, when he was a-dying, bade God bless us, and prayed that if grand-father lived he might send him to support us."

"Where did they lay my boy?" said Edwards.

"In the Old Churchyard," replied the woman, "hard by his mother."

"I will show it you," answered the boy, "for I have wept over it many a time when first I came among strange folks."

He took the old man's hand, Harley laid hold of his sister's, and they walked in silence to the churchyard.

There was an old stone, with the corner broken off, and some letters, half-covered with moss, to denote the names of the dead: there was a cyphered R. E. plainer than the rest; it was the tomb they sought.

"Here it is, grandfather," said the boy.

Edwards gazed upon it without uttering a word: the girl, who had only sighed before, now wept outright; her brother sobbed, but he stifled his sobbing.

"I have told sister," said he, "that she should not take it so to heart; she can knit already, and I shall soon be able to dig, we shall not starve, sister, indeed we shall not, nor shall grandfather neither."

The girl cried afresh; Harley kissed off her tears as they flowed, and wept between every kiss.

CHAPTER XXXVI

HE RETURNS HOME—A DESCRIPTION OF HIS RETINUE

IT was with some difficulty that Harley prevailed on the old man to leave the spot where the remains of his son were laid. At last, with the assistance of the school-mistress, he prevailed; and she accommodated Edwards and him with beds in her house, there being nothing like an inn nearer than the distance of some miles.

In the morning Harley persuaded Edwards to come with the children to his house, which was distant but a short day's journey. The boy walked in his grandfather's hand; and the name of Edwards procured him a neighbouring farmer's horse, on which a servant mounted, with the girl on a pillow before him.

With this train Harley returned to the abode of his fathers: and we cannot but think, that his enjoyment was as great as if he had arrived from the tour of Europe with a Swiss valet for his companion, and half a dozen snuff-boxes, with invisible hinges, in his pocket. But we take our ideas from sounds which folly has invented; Fashion, Bon ton, and Vertù, are the names of certain idols, to which we sacrifice the genuine pleasures of the soul: in this world of semblance, we are contented with personating happiness; to feel it is an art beyond us.

It was otherwise with Harley; he ran upstairs to his aunt with the history of his fellow-travellers glowing on his lips. His aunt was an economist; but she knew the pleasure of doing charitable things, and withal was fond of her nephew, and solicitous to oblige him. She received old Edwards therefore with a look of more complacency than is perhaps natural to maiden ladies of three-score, and was remarkably attentive to his grandchildren: she roasted apples with her own hands for their supper, and made up a little bed beside her own for the girl. Edwards made some attempts towards an acknowledgment for these favours; but his young friend stopped them in their beginnings.

" Whosoever receiveth any of these children," said his aunt; for her acquaintance with her Bible was habitual.

Early next morning Harley stole into the room where Edwards lay: he expected to have found him a-bed, but in this he was mistaken: the old man had risen, and was leaning over his sleeping grandson, with the tears flowing down his cheeks. At first he did not perceive Harley; when he did, he endeavoured to hide his grief, and crossing his eyes with his hand expressed his surprise at seeing him so early astir.

" I was thinking of you," said Harley, " and your children: I learned last night that a small farm of mine in the neighbourhood is now vacant: if you will occupy it I shall gain a good neighbour and be able in some measure to repay the notice you took of me when a boy, and as the furniture of the house is mine, it will be so much trouble saved."

Edwards' tears gushed afresh, and Harley led him to see the place he intended for him.

The house upon this farm was indeed little better than a hut; its situation, however, was pleasant, and Edwards, assisted by the beneficence of Harley, set about improving its neatness and convenience. He staked out a piece of the green before for a garden, and Peter, who acted in Harley's family as valet, butler, and gardener, had orders to furnish him with parcels of the different seeds he chose to sow in it. I have seen his master at work in this little spot with his coat off, and his dibble in his hand: it was a scene of tranquil virtue to have stopped an angel on his errands of mercy! Harley had contrived to lead a little bubbling brook through a green walk in the middle of the ground, upon which he had erected a mill in miniature for the diversion of Edwards' infant grandson, and made shift in its construction to introduce a pliant bit of wood that answered with its fairy clack to the murmuring of the rill that turned it. I have seen him stand, listening to these mingled sounds, with his eye fixed on the boy, and the smile of conscious satisfaction on his cheek, while the old man, with a look half turned to Harley and half to heaven, breathed an ejaculation of gratitude and piety.

Father of mercies! I also would thank thee that not only hast thou assigned eternal rewards to virtue, but that, even in this bad world, the lines of our duty and our happiness are so frequently woven together.

THE MAN OF FEELING

A FRAGMENT

* * "EDWARDS," said he, "I have a proper regard for the prosperity of my country: every native of it appropriates to himself some share of the power, or the fame, which, as a nation, it acquires, but I cannot throw off the man so much as to rejoice at our conquests in India. You tell me of immense territories subject to the English: I cannot think of their possessions without being led to inquire by what right they possess them. They came there as traders, bartering the commodities they brought for others which their purchasers could spare; and however great their profits were, they were then equitable. But what title have the subjects of another kingdom to establish an empire in India? to give laws to a country where the inhabitants received them on the terms of friendly commerce? You say they are happier under our regulations than under the tyranny of their own petty princes. I must doubt it, from the conduct of those by whom these regulations have been made. They have drained the treasuries of Nabobs, who must fill them by oppressing the industry of their subjects. Nor is this to be wondered at, when we consider the motive upon which those gentlemen do not deny their going to India. The fame of conquest, barbarous as that motive is, is but a secondary consideration: there are certain stations in wealth, as well as in rank and honour, to which the warriors of the East aspire. It is there, indeed, where the wishes of their friends assign them eminence, and to that object the question of their country is pointed at their return. When shall I see a commander return from India in the pride of honourable poverty? You describe the victories they have gained; they are sullied by the cause in which they fought: you enumerate the spoils of those victories; they are covered with the blood of the vanquished.

"Could you tell me of some conqueror giving peace and happiness to the conquered? did he accept the gifts of their princes to use them for the comfort of those whose fathers, sons, or husbands, fell in battle? did he use his power to gain security and freedom to the regions of oppression and slavery? did he endear the British name by examples of generosity, which the most barbarous or most depraved are rarely able to resist? did he return with the consciousness of duty discharged to his country, and humanity to his fellow-creatures? did he return with no lace on his coat, no slaves in his retinue, no chariot at his door, and no burgundy at his table?—these were laurels which princes might envy—which an honest man would not condemn!"

"Your maxims, Mr. Harley, are certainly right," said Edwards. "I am not capable of arguing with you; but I imagine there are great temptations in a great degree of riches, which it is no easy matter to resist: those a poor man like me cannot describe, because he never knew them; and perhaps I have reason to bless God that I never did; for then, it is likely, I should have withstood them no better than my neighbours. For you know, sir, that it is not the fashion now, as it was in former times, that I have read of in books, when your great generals died so poor, that they did not leave wherewithal to buy them a coffin; and people thought the better of their memories for it: if they did so now-a-days, I question if any body, except yourself, and some few like you, would thank them."

"I am sorry," replied Harley, "that there is so much truth in what you say; but however the general current of opinion may point, the feelings are not yet lost that applaud benevolence, and censure inhumanity. Let us endeavour to strengthen them in ourselves; and we, who live sequestered from the noise of the multitude, have better opportunities of listening undisturbed to their voice."

They now approached the little dwelling of Edwards. A maid-servant, whom he had hired to assist him in the care of his grandchildren, met them a little way from the house: "There is a young lady within with the children," said she. Edwards expressed his surprise at the visit: it was however not the less true; and we mean to account for it.

This young lady then was no other than Miss Walton. She had heard the old man's history from Harley, as we have already related it. Curiosity, or some other motive, made her desirous to see his grandchildren; this she had an opportunity of gratifying soon, the children, in some of their walks, having strolled as far as her father's avenue. She put several questions to both; she was delighted with the simplicity of their answers, and promised, that if they continued to be good children, and do as their grandfather bid them, she would soon see them again, and bring some present or other for their reward. This promise she had performed now: she came attended only by her maid, and brought with her a complete suit of green for the boy, and a chintz gown, a cap, and a suit of ribands, for his sister. She had time enough, with her maid's assistance, to equip them in their new habiliments before Harley and Edwards returned. The boy heard his grandfather's voice, and, with that silent joy which his present finery inspired, ran to the door to meet him: putting one hand in his, with the other pointing to his sister, "See," said he, "what Miss Walton has brought us?"—Edwards gazed on them. Harley fixed his eyes on Miss Walton; hers were turned to the ground;—in Edwards' was a beamy moisture.—He folded his hands together——"I cannot speak, young lady," said he, "to thank you." Neither could Harley. There were a thousand sentiments; but they gushed so impetuously on his heart, that he could not utter a syllable. * *

CHAPTER XL

THE MAN OF FEELING JEALOUS

THE desire of communicating knowledge or intelligence, is an argument with those who hold that man is naturally a social animal. It is indeed one of the earliest propensities we discover; but it may be doubted whether the pleasure (for pleasure there certainly is) arising from it be not often more selfish than social: for we frequently observe the tidings of Ill communicated as eagerly as the annunciation of Good. Is it that we delight in observing the effects of the stronger passions? for we are all philosophers in this respect; and it is perhaps amongst the spectators at Tyburn that the most genuine are to be found.

Was it from this motive that Peter came one morning into

his master's room with a meaning face of recital? His master indeed did not at first observe it; for he was sitting with one shoe buckled, delineating portraits in the fire. "I have brushed those clothes, sir, as you ordered me."——Harley nodded his head; but Peter observed that his hat wanted brushing too: his master nodded again. At last Peter bethought him that the fire needed stirring; and taking up the poker, demolished the turban'd head of a Saracen, while his master was seeking out a body for it. "The morning is main cold, sir," said Peter. "Is it?" said Harley. "Yes, sir; I have been as far as Tom Dowson's to fetch some barberries he had picked for Mrs. Margery. There was a rare junketting last night at Thomas's among Sir Harry Benson's servants; he lay at Squire Walton's, but he would not suffer his servants to trouble the family: so, to be sure, they were all at Tom's, and had a fiddle, and a hot supper in the big room where the justices meet about the destroying of hares and partridges, and them things; and Tom's eyes looked so red and so bleared when I called him to get the barberries:—And I hear as how Sir Harry is going to be married to Miss Walton."——"How! Miss Walton married!" said Harley. "Why, it mayn't be true, sir, for all that; but Tom's wife told it me, and to be sure the servants told her, and their master told them, as I guess, sir; but it mayn't be true for all that, as I said before."—"Have done with your idle information," said Harley:—"Is my aunt come down into the parlour to breakfast?"—"Yes, sir."—"Tell her I'll be with her immediately."

When Peter was gone, he stood with his eyes fixed on the ground, and the last words of his intelligence vibrating in his ears. "Miss Walton married!" he sighed—and walked down stairs, with his shoe as it was, and the buckle in his hand. His aunt, however, was pretty well accustomed to those appearances of absence; besides, that the natural gravity of her temper, which was commonly called into exertion by the care of her household concerns, was such as not easily to be discomposed by any circumstance of accidental impropriety. She too had been informed of the intended match between Sir Harry Benson and Miss Walton. "I have been thinking," said she, "that they are distant relations: for the great-grandfather of this Sir Harry Benson, who was knight of the shire in the reign of Charles the First, and one of the cavaliers of those times, was married to a daughter of the Walton family." Harley answered drily, that it might be so; but that he never troubled himself about those matters. "Indeed," said she, "you are to blame, nephew, for not knowing a little more of them: before I was near your age I had sewed the pedigree of our family in a set of chair-bottoms, that were made a present of to my grandmother, who was a very notable woman, and had a proper regard for gentility, I'll assure you; but now-a-days it is money, not birth, that makes people respected; the more shame for the times."

Harley was in no very good humour for entering into a discussion of this question; but he always entertained so much filial respect for his aunt, as to attend to her discourse.

"We blame the pride of the rich," said he, "but are not we ashamed of our poverty?"

"Why, one would not choose," replied his aunt, "to make a much worse figure than one's neighbours; but, as I was saying before, the times (as my friend, Mrs. Dorothy Walton, observes) are shamefully degenerated in this respect. There was but t'other day at Mr. Walton's, that fat fellow's daughter, the London merchant, as he calls himself, though I have heard that he was little better than the keeper of a chandler's shop. We were leaving the gentlemen to go to tea. She had a hoop, forsooth, as large and as stiff—and it showed a pair of bandy legs, as thick as two——I was nearer the door by an apron's length, and the pert hussy brushed by me, as who should say, Make way for your betters, and with one of her London bobs—but Mrs. Dorothy did not let her pass with it: for all the time of drinking tea, she spoke of the precedency of family, and the disparity there is between people who are come of something and your mushroom gentry who wear their coats of arms in their purses."

Her indignation was interrupted by the arrival of her maid with a damask table-cloth, and a set of napkins, from the loom, which had been spun by her mistress's own hand. There was the family crest in each corner, and in the middle a view of the battle of Worcester, where one of her ancestors had been a captain in the king's forces; and with a sort of poetical licence in perspective, there was seen the Royal Oak, with more wig than leaves upon it.

On all this the good lady was very copious, and took up the remaining intervals of filling tea, 'to describe its excellencies to Harley; adding, that she intended this as a present for his wife, when he should get one. He sighed and looked foolish, and commending the serenity of the day, walked out into the garden.

He sat down on a little seat which commanded an extensive prospect round the house. He leaned on his hand, and scored the ground with his stick: " Miss Walton married! " said he; " but what is that to me? May she be happy! her virtues deserve it; to me her marriage is otherwise indifferent: I had romantic dreams? they are fled?—it is perfectly indifferent."

Just at that moment he saw a servant with a knot of ribbons in his hat go into the house. His cheeks grew flushed at the sight! He kept his eye fixed for some time on the door by which he had entered, then starting to his feet, hastily followed him.

When he approached the door of the kitchen where he supposed the man had entered, his heart throbbed so violently, that when he would have called Peter, his voice failed in the attempt. He stood a moment listening in this breathless state of palpitation: Peter came out by chance. " Did your honour want any thing? "—" Where is the servant that came just now from Mr. Walton's? "——" From Mr. Walton's, sir! there is none of his servants here that I know of."—" Nor of Sir Harry Benson's? "—He did not wait for an answer; but having by this time observed the hat with its parti-coloured ornament hanging on a peg near the door, he pressed forwards into the kitchen, and addressing himself to a stranger whom he saw there, asked him, with no small tremor in his voice, " If he had any commands for him? " The man looked silly, and said, " That he had nothing to trouble his honour with." —" Are not you a servant of Sir Harry Benson's? "—" No, sir."—" You'll pardon me, young man; I judged by the favour in your hat."—" Sir, I'm his majesty's servant, God bless him! and these favours we always wear when we are recruiting."—" Recruiting! " his eyes glistened at the word: he seized the soldier's hand, and shaking it violently, ordered

Peter to fetch a bottle of his aunt's best dram. The bottle was brought: "You shall drink the king's health," said Harley, "in a bumper."——"The king and your honour."——"Nay, you shall drink the king's health by itself; you may drink mine in another." Peter looked in his master's face, and filled with some little reluctance. "Now to your mistress," said Harley; "every soldier has a mistress." The man excused himself—"To your mistress! you cannot refuse it." 'Twas Mrs. Margery's best dram! Peter stood with the bottle a little inclined, but not so as to discharge a drop of its contents: "Fill it, Peter," said his master, "fill it to the brim." Peter filled it; and the soldier having named Suky Simpson, dispatched it in a twinkling. "Thou art an honest fellow," said Harley, "and I love thee;" and shaking his hand again desired Peter to make him his guest at dinner, and walked up into his room with a pace much quicker and more springy than usual.

This agreeable disappointment, however, he was not long suffered to enjoy. The curate happened that day to dine with him: his visits, indeed, were more properly to the aunt than the nephew; and many of the intelligent ladies in the parish, who, like some very great philosophers, have the happy knack at accounting for everything, gave out that there was a particular attachment between them, which wanted only to be matured by some more years of courtship to end in the tenderest connection. In this conclusion, indeed, supposing the premises to have been true, they were somewhat justified by the known opinion of the lady, who frequently declared herself a friend to the ceremonial of former times, when a lover might have sighed seven years at his mistress's feet before he was allowed the liberty of kissing her hand. 'Tis true Mrs. Margery was now about her grand climacteric; no matter: that is just the age when we expect to grow younger. But I verily believe there was nothing in the report; the curate's connection was only that of a genealogist; for in that character he was no way inferior to Mrs. Margery herself. He dealt also in the present times; for he was a politician and a news-monger.

He had hardly said grace after dinner, when he told Mrs. Margery that she might soon expect a pair of white gloves, as

THE MAN OF FEELING

Sir Harry Benson, he was very well informed, was just going to be married to Miss Walton. Harley spilt the wine he was carrying to his mouth: he had time, however, to recollect himself before the curate had finished the different particulars of his intelligence, and summoning up all the heroism he was master of, filled a bumper, and drank to Miss Walton. "With all my heart," said the curate, "the bride that is to be." Harley would have said bride too; but the word bride stuck in his throat. His confusion, indeed, was manifest; but the curate began to enter on some point of descent with Mrs. Margery, and Harley had very soon after an opportunity of leaving them, while they were deeply engaged in a question, whether the name of some great man in the time of Henry the Seventh was Richard or Humphrey.

He did not see his aunt again till supper; the time between he spent in walking, like some troubled ghost, round the place where his treasure lay. He went as far as a little gate, that led into a copse near Mr. Walton's house, to which that gentleman had been so obliging as to let him have a key. He had just begun to open it when he saw, on a terrace below, Miss Walton walking with a gentleman in a riding-dress, whom he immediately guessed to be Sir Harry Benson. He stopped of a sudden; his hand shook so much that he could hardly turn the key; he opened the gate, however, and advanced a few paces. The lady's lap-dog pricked up its ears, and barked; he stopped again—

> —————"The little dogs and all,
> Tray, Blanch, and Sweetheart, see they bark at me!"

His resolution failed; he slunk back, and, locking the gate as softly as he could, stood on tiptoe looking over the wall till they were gone. At that instant a shepherd blew his horn: the romantic melancholy of the sound quite overcame him!—it was the very note that wanted to be touched—he sighed! he dropped a tear!—and returned.

At supper his aunt observed that he was graver than usual; but she did not suspect the cause: indeed, it may seem odd that she was the only person in the family who had no suspicion of his attachment to Miss Walton. It was frequently matter of

discourse amongst the servants: perhaps her maiden coldness
—but for those things we need not account.

In a day or two he was so much master of himself as to be
able to rhyme upon the subject. The following pastoral he
left, some time after, on the handle of a tea-kettle, at a neighbouring house where we were visiting; and as I filled the tea-
pot after him, I happened to put it in my pocket by a similar
act of forgetfulness. It is such as might be expected from a
man who makes verses for amusement. I am pleased with
somewhat of good nature that runs through it, because I have
commonly observed the writers of those complaints to bestow
epithets on their lost mistresses rather too harsh for the mere
liberty of choice, which led them to prefer another to the poet
himself: I do not doubt the vehemence of their passion; but,
alas! the sensations of love are something more than the returns of gratitude.

LAVINIA.

A PASTORAL.

Why steals from my bosom the sigh?
  Why fixed is my gaze on the ground?
Come, give me my pipe, and I'll try
  To banish my cares with the sound.

Erewhile were its notes of accord
  With the smile of the flow'r-footed Muse;
Ah! why by its master implored
  Shou'd it now the gay carol refuse?

'Twas taught by LAVINIA's smile,
  In the mirth-loving chorus to join:
Ah, me! how unweeting the while!
  LAVINIA——cannot be mine!

Another, more happy, the maid
  By fortune is destin'd to bless——
'Tho' the hope has forsook that betray'd,
  Yet why should I love her the less?

Her beauties are bright as the morn,
  With rapture I counted them o'er;
Such virtues these beauties adorn,
  I knew her, and prais'd them no more.

THE MAN OF FEELING

I term'd her no goddess of love,
　　I call'd not her beauty divine:
These far other passions may prove,
　　But they could not be figures of mine.

It ne'er was apparel'd with art,
　　On words it could never rely;
It reign'd in the throb of my heart,
　　It spoke in the glance of my eye.

Oh fool! in the circle to shine
　　That Fashion's gay daughters approve
You must speak as the fashions incline;
　　Alas! are there fashions in love?

Yet sure they are simple who prize
　　The tongue that is smooth to deceive;
Yet sure she had sense to despise,
　　The tinsel that folly may weave.

When I talk'd, I have seen her recline,
　　With an aspect so pensively sweet,—
Tho' I spoke what the shepherds opine,
　　A fop were ashamed to repeat.

She is soft as the dew-drops that fall
　　From the lip of the sweet-scented pea;
Perhaps when she smil'd upon all,
　　I have thought that she smil'd upon me.

But why of her charms should I tell?
　　Ah me! whom her charms have undone
Yet I love the reflection too well,
　　The painful reflection to shun.

Ye souls of more delicate kind,
　　Who feast not on pleasure alone,
Who wear the soft sense of the mind,
　　To the sons of the world still unknown.

Ye know, tho' I cannot express,
　　Why I foolishly doat on my pain;
Nor will ye believe it the less,
　　That I have not the skill to complain.

I lean on my hand with a sigh,
　　My friends the soft sadness condemn;
Yet, methinks, tho' I cannot tell why,
　　I should hate to be merry like them.

THE MAN OF FEELING

When I walk'd in the pride of the dawn,
  Methought all the region look'd bright:
Has sweetness forsaken the lawn?
  For, methinks, I grow sad at the sight.

When I stood by the stream, I have thought
  There was mirth in the gurgling soft sound;
But now 'tis a sorrowful note,
  And the banks are all gloomy around!

I have laugh'd at the jest of a friend;
  Now they laugh, and I know not the cause,
Tho' I seem with my looks to attend,
  How silly! I ask what it was.

They sing the sweet song of the May,
  They sing it with mirth and with glee;
Sure I once thought the sonnet was gay,
  But now 'tis all sadness to me.

Oh! give me the dubious light
  That gleams thro' the quivering shade;
Oh! give me the horrors of night,
  By gloom and by silence array'd!

Let me walk where the soft-rising wave,
  Has pictur'd the moon on its breast;
Let me walk where the new cover'd grave
  Allows the pale lover to rest!

When shall I in its peaceable womb,
  Be laid with my sorrows asleep!
Should LAVINIA chance on my tomb—
  I could die if I thought she would weep.

Perhaps, if the souls of the just
  Revisit these mansions of care,
It may be my favourite trust
  To watch o'er the fate of the fair.

Perhaps the soft thought of her breast,
  With rapture more favour'd to warm;
Perhaps, if with sorrow oppress'd,
  Her sorrow with patience to arm.

Then, then, in the tenderest part
  May I whisper, " Poor COLIN was true,"
And mark if a heave of her heart
  The thought of her COLIN pursue.

THE PUPIL

A FRAGMENT

* * " **B**UT as to the higher part of education, Mr. Harley, the culture of the mind—let the feelings be awakened, let the heart be brought forward to its object, placed in the light in which nature would have it stand, and its decisions will ever be just. The world

> Will smile, and smile, and be a villain;

and the youth, who does not suspect its deceit, will be content to smile with it. His teachers will put on the most forbidding aspect in nature, and tell him of the beauty of virtue.

" I have not, under these grey hairs, forgotten that I was once a young man, warm in the pursuit of pleasure, but meaning to be honest as well as happy. I had ideas of virtue, of honour, of benevolence, which I had never been at the pains to define; but I felt my bosom heave at the thoughts of them, and I made the most delightful soliloquies. It is impossible, said I, that there can be half so many rogues as are imagined.

" I travelled, because it is the fashion for young men of my fortune to travel. I had a travelling tutor, which is the fashion too; but my tutor was a gentleman, which it is not always the fashion for tutors to be. His gentility, indeed, was all he had from his father, whose prodigality had not left him a shilling to support it.

" ' I have a favor to ask of you, my dear Mountford,' said my father, ' which I will not be refused. You have travelled as became a man; neither France nor Italy have made anything of Mountford, which Mountford, before he left England, would have been ashamed of. My son Edward goes abroad, would you take him under your protection?'

" He blushed; my father's face was scarlet. He pressed his hand to his bosom, as if he had said, my heart does not mean to offend you. Mountford sighed twice.

" ' I am a proud fool,' said he, ' and you will pardon it. There! (he sighed again) I can hear of dependence, since it is dependence on my Sedley.'

" ' Dependence!' answered my father; ' there can be no

such word between us. What is there in £9,000 a year that should make me unworthy of Mountford's friendship?'

" They embraced; and soon after I set out on my travels, with Mountford for my guardian.

" We were at Milan, where my father happened to have an Italian friend, to whom he had been of some service in England. The count, for he was of quality, was solicitous to return the obligation by a particular attention to his son. We lived in his palace, visited with his family, were caressed by his friends, and I began to be so well pleased with my entertainment, that I thought of England as of some foreign country.

" The count had a son not much older than myself. At that age a friend is an easy acquisition; we were friends the first night of our acquaintance.

" He introduced me into the company of a set of young gentlemen, whose fortunes gave them the command of pleasure, and whose inclinations incited them to the purchase. After having spent some joyous evenings in their society, it became a sort of habit which I could not miss without uneasiness, and our meetings, which before were frequent, were now stated and regular.

" Sometimes, in the pauses of our mirth, gaming was introduced as an amusement. It was an art in which I was a novice. I received instruction, as other novices do, by losing pretty largely to my teachers. Nor was this the only evil which Mountford foresaw would arise from the connection I had formed; but a lecture of sour injunctions was not his method of reclaiming. He sometimes asked me questions about the company, but they were such as the curiosity of any indifferent man might have prompted. I told him of their wit, their eloquence, their warmth of friendship, and their sensibility of heart. ' And their honour,' said I, laying my hand on my breast, ' is unquestionable.' Mountford seemed to rejoice at my good fortune, and begged that I would introduce him to their acquaintance. At the next meeting I introduced him accordingly.

" The conversation was as animated as usual. They displayed all that sprightliness and good-humour which my praises had led Mountford to expect; subjects, too, of sentiment occurred, and their speeches, particularly those of our friend the son of Count Respino, glowed with the warmth of honour, and softened into the tenderness of feeling. Mountford was charmed with his companions. When we parted, he made the highest eulogiums upon them. ' When shall we see them again?' said he. I was delighted with the demand, and promised to reconduct him on the morrow.

" In going to their place of rendezvous, he took me a little out of the road, to see, as he told me, the performances of a young statuary. When we were near the house in which Mountford said he lived, a boy of about seven years old crossed us in the street. At sight of Mountford he stopped, and grasping his hand,

" ' My dearest sir,' said he, ' my father is likely to do well. He will live to pray for you, and to bless you. Yes, he will bless you, though you are an Englishman, and some other hard word that the monk talked of this morning, which I have forgot, but it meant that you should not go to heaven; but he shall go to heaven, said I, for he has saved my father. Come and see him, sir, that we may be happy.'

" ' My dear, I am engaged at present with this gentleman.'

" ' But he shall come along with you; he is an Englishman, too, I fancy. He shall come and learn how an Englishman may go to heaven.'

" Mountford smiled, and we followed the boy together.

" After crossing the next street, we arrived at the gate of a prison. I seemed surprised at the sight; our little conductor observed it.

" ' Are you afraid, sir?' said he. ' I was afraid once too, but my father and mother are here, and I am never afraid when I am with them.'

" He took my hand, and led me through a dark passage that fronted the gate. When we came to a little door at the end, he tapped. A boy, still younger than himself, opened it to receive us. Mountford entered with a look in which was pictured the benign assurance of a superior being. I followed in silence and amazement.

" On something like a bed, lay a man, with a face seemingly emaciated with sickness, and a look of patient dejection. A bundle of dirty shreds served him for a pillow, but he had a better support—the arm of a female who kneeled beside him, beautiful as an angel, but with a fading languor in her countenance, the still life of melancholy, that seemed to borrow its shade from the object on which she gazed. There was a tear in her eye—the sick man kissed it off in its bud, smiling through the dimness of his own—when she saw Mountford, she crawled forward on the ground, and clasped his knees. He raised her from the floor; she threw her arms round his neck, and sobbed out a speech of thankfulness, eloquent beyond the power of language.

"'Compose yourself, my love,' said the man on the bed; 'but he, whose goodness has caused that emotion, will pardon its effects.'

"'How is this, Mountford?' said I; 'what do I see? What must I do?'

"'You see,' replied the stranger, 'a wretch, sunk in poverty, starving in prison, stretched on a sick bed. But that is little. There are his wife and children wanting the bread which he has not to give them! Yet you cannot easily imagine the conscious serenity of his mind. In the gripe of affliction, his heart swells with the pride of virtue; it can even look down with pity on the man whose cruelty has wrung it almost to bursting. You are, I fancy, a friend of Mr. Mountford's. Come nearer, and I'll tell you, for, short as my story is, I can hardly command breath enough for a recital. The son of Count Respino (I started, as if I had trod on a viper) has long had a criminal passion for my wife. This her prudence had concealed from me; but he had lately the boldness to declare it to myself. He promised me affluence in exchange for honour, and threatened misery as its attendant if I kept it. I treated him with the contempt he deserved; the consequence was, that he hired a couple of bravoes (for I am persuaded they acted under his direction), who attempted to assassinate me in the street; but I made such a defence as obliged them to fly, after having given me two or three stabs, none of which, however, were mortal. But his revenge was not thus to be disappointed. In the little dealings of my trade I had contracted some debts, of which he had made himself master for my ruin. I was confined here at his suit. when not yet recovered from the wounds I had received; this dear woman, and these two boys, followed me, that we might starve together; but Providence interposed, and sent Mr. Mountford to our support. He has relieved my family from the gnawings of hunger, and rescued me from death, to which a fever, consequent on my wounds and increased by the want of every necessary, had almost reduced me.'

"" Inhuman villain!' I exclaimed, lifting up my eyes to heaven.

" ' Inhuman indeed!' said the lovely woman who stood at my side. ' Alas! sir, what had we done to offend him? what had these little ones done, that they should perish in the toils of his vengeance?'

" I reached a pen which stood in the ink-standish at the bed-side.

" ' May I ask what is the amount of the sum for which you are imprisoned?'

" ' I was able,' he replied, ' to pay all but five hundred crowns.'

" I wrote a draft on the banker with whom I had a credit from my father for 2,500, and presenting it to the stranger's wife,

" ' You will receive, madam, on presenting this note, a sum more than sufficient for your husband's discharge; the remainder I leave for his industry to improve.'

" I would have left the room. Each of them laid hold of one of my hands, the children clung to my coat. Oh! Mr. Harley, methinks I feel their gentle violence at this moment; it beats here with delight inexpressible.

" ' Stay, sir,' said he, ' I do not mean attempting to thank you ' (he took a pocket-book from under his pillow), ' let me but know what name I shall place here next to Mr. Mountford?'

" ' Sedley.'

" He writ it down.

" ' An Englishman too, I presume.'

" ' He shall go to heaven, notwithstanding,' said the boy who had been our guide.

" It began to be too much for me. I squeezed his hand that was clasped in mine, his wife's I pressed to my lips, and burst from the place, to give vent to the feelings that laboured within me.

" 'Oh, Mountford!' said I, when he had overtaken me at the door.

" 'It is time,' replied he, 'that we should think of our appointment; young Respino and his friends are waiting us.'

" 'Damn him, damn him!' said I. 'Let us leave Milan instantly; but soft—I will be calm; Mountford, your pencil.' I wrote on a slip of paper,

" 'To Signor RESPINO.

" 'When you receive this, I am at a distance from Milan. Accept of my thanks for the civilities I have received from you and your family. As to the friendship with which you were pleased to honour me, the prison, which I have just left, has exhibited a scene to cancel it for ever. You may possibly be merry with your companions at my weakness, as I suppose you will term it. I give you leave for derision. You may affect a triumph, I shall feel it.

" 'EDWARD SEDLEY.'

" 'You may send this if you will,' said Mountford, coolly, 'but still Respino is *a man of honour;* the world will continue to call him so.'

" 'It is probable,' I answered, 'they may; I envy not the appellation. If this is the world's honour, if these men are the guides of its manners——'

" 'Tut!' said Mountford, 'do you eat macaroni——' "

*   *   *   *   *   *

[At this place had the greatest depredations of the curate begun. There were so very few connected passages of the subsequent chapters remaining, that even the partiality of an editor could not offer them to the public. I discovered, from some scattered sentences, that they were of much the same tenor with the preceding; recitals of little adventures, in which the dispositions of a man, sensible to judge, and still more warm to feel, had room to unfold themselves. Some instruction, and some example, I make no doubt they contained; but it is likely that many of those, whom chance has led to a perusal of what I have already presented, may have read it with little pleasure, and will feel no disappointment from the want of those parts which I have been unable to procure. To such as may have expected the intricacies of a novel, a few incidents in a life undistinguished, except by some features of the heart, cannot have afforded much entertainment.

Harley's own story, from the mutilated passages I have mentioned, as well as from some inquiries I was at the trouble of making in the country, I found to have been simple to excess. His mistress, I could perceive, was not married to Sir Harry Benson; but it would seem, by one of the following chapters, which is still entire, that Harley had not profited on the occasion by making any declaration of his own passion, after those of the other had been unsuccessful. The state of his health, for some part of this period, appears to have been such as to forbid any thoughts of that kind : he had been seized with a very dangerous fever, caught by attending old Edwards in one of an infectious kind. From this he had recovered but imperfectly, and though he had no formed complaint, his health was manifestly on the decline.

It appears that the sagacity of some friend had at length pointed out to his aunt a cause from which this might be supposed to proceed, to wit, his hopeless love for Miss Walton; for, according to the conceptions of the world, the love of a man of Harley's fortune for the heiress of £4,000 a year is indeed desperate. Whether it was so in this case may be gathered from the next chapter, which, with the two subsequent, concluding the performance, have escaped those accidents that proved fatal to the rest.]

CHAPTER LV

HE SEES MISS WALTON, AND IS HAPPY

HARLEY was one of those few friends whom the malevolence of fortune had yet left me; I could not therefore but be sensibly concerned for his present indisposition; there seldom passed a day on which I did not make inquiry about him.

The physician who attended him had informed me the evening before, that he thought him considerably better than he had been for some time past. I called next morning to be confirmed in a piece of intelligence so welcome to me.

When I entered his apartment, I found him sitting on a couch, leaning on his hand, with his eye turned upwards in the attitude of thoughtful inspiration. His look had always an open benignity, which commanded esteem; there was now something more—a gentle triumph in it.

He rose, and met me with his usual kindness. When I gave him the good accounts I had had from his physician, " I am foolish enough," said he, " to rely but little, in this instance, upon physic: my presentiment may be false; but I think I feel myself approaching to my end, by steps so easy, that they woo me to approach it.

" There is a certain dignity in retiring from life at a time, when the infirmities of age have not sapped our faculties. This world, my dear Charles, was a scene in which I never much delighted. I was not formed for the bustle of the busy, nor the dissipation of the gay; a thousand things occurred, where I blushed for the impropriety of my conduct when I thought on the world, though my reason told me I should have blushed to have done otherwise.—It was a scene of dissimulation, of restraint, of disappointment. I leave it to enter on that state which I have learned to believe is replete with the genuine happiness attendant upon virtue. I look back on the tenor of my life, with the consciousness of few great offences to account for. There are blemishes, I confess, which deform in some degree the picture. But I know the benignity of the Supreme Being, and rejoice at the thoughts of its exercises in my favour. My mind expands at the thought I shall enter into the society of the blessed, wise as angels, with the simplicity of children." He had by this time clasped my hand, and found it wet by a tear which had just fallen upon it.— His eye began to moisten too—we sat for some time silent.— At last, with an attempt to a look of more composure, " There are some remembrances," said Harley, " which rise involuntarily on my heart, and make me almost wish to live. I have been blessed with a few friends, who redeem my opinion of mankind. I recollect, with the tenderest emotion, the scenes of pleasure I have passed among them; but we shall meet again, my friend, never to be separated. There are some feelings which perhaps are too tender to be suffered by the world. The world is in general selfish, interested, and unthinking, and throws the imputation of romance or melancholy on every temper more susceptible than its own. I cannot think but in those regions which I contemplate, if there is any thing of mortality left about us, that these feelings will subsist;—they are called,—perhaps they are—weaknesses here;—but there may be some better modifications of them in heaven, which may deserve the name of virtues." He sighed as he spoke these last words. He had scarcely finished them, when the door opened, and his aunt appeared, leading in Miss Walton. "My dear," says she, "here is Miss Walton, who has been so kind as to come and inquire for you herself." I could observe a transient glow upon his face. He rose from his seat—"If to know Miss Walton's goodness," said he, "be a title to deserve it, I have some claim." She begged him to resume his seat, and placed herself on the sofa beside him. I took my leave. Mrs. Margery accompanied me to the door. He was left with Miss Walton alone. She inquired anxiously about his health. "I believe," said he, "from the accounts which my physicians unwillingly give me, that they have no great hopes of my recovery."—She started as he spoke; but recollecting herself immediately, endeavoured to flatter him into a belief that his apprehensions were groundless. "I know," said he, "that it is usual with persons at my time of life to have these hopes, which your kindness suggests; but I would not wish to be deceived. To meet death as becomes a man, is a privilege bestowed on few.—I would endeavour to make it mine;—nor do I think that I can ever be better prepared for it than now:—It is that chiefly which determines the fitness of its approach." "Those sentiments," answered Miss Walton, "are just; but your good sense, Mr. Harley, will own, that life has its proper value.—As the province of virtue, life is ennobled; as such, it is to be desired.—To virtue has the Supreme Director of all things assigned rewards enough even here to fix its attachment."

The subject began to overpower her.—Harley lifted his eyes from the ground—"There are," said he, in a very low voice, "there are attachments, Miss Walton"—His glance met hers.—They both betrayed a confusion, and were both instantly withdrawn.—He paused some moments—" I am in such a state as calls for sincerity, let that also excuse it—It is perhaps the last time we shall ever meet. I feel something particularly solemn in the acknowledgment, yet my heart swells to make it, awed as it is by a sense of my presumption, by a sense of your perfections "—He paused again——" Let it not offend you, to know their power over one so unworthy— It will, I believe, soon cease to beat, even with that feeling which it shall lose the latest.—To love Miss Walton could not be a crime;—if to declare it is one—the expiation will be made."—Her tears were now flowing without control.—" Let me intreat you," said she, " to have better hopes—Let not life be so indifferent to you; if my wishes can put any value on it —I will not pretend to misunderstand you—I know your worth—I have known it long—I have esteemed it—What would you have me say?—I have loved it as it deserved."— He seized her hand—a languid colour reddened his cheek—a smile brightened faintly in his eye. As he gazed on her, it grew dim, it fixed, it closed—He sighed and fell back on his seat—Miss Walton screamed at the sight—His aunt and the servants rushed into the room—They found them lying motionless together.—His physician happened to call at that instant. Every art was tried to recover them—With Miss Walton they succeeded—But Harley was gone for ever.

———

CHAPTER LVI

THE EMOTIONS OF THE HEART

I ENTERED the room where his body lay; I approached it with reverence, not fear: I looked; the recollection of the past crowded upon me. I saw that form which, but a little before, was animated with a soul which did honour to humanity, stretched without sense or feeling before me. 'Tis a connection we cannot easily forget:—I took his hand in mine; I repeated his name involuntarily;—I felt a pulse in every vein at the sound. I looked earnestly in his face; his eye was closed, his lip pale and motionless. There is an enthusiasm in sorrow that forgets impossibility; I wondered that it was so. The sight drew a prayer from my heart: it was the voice of frailty and of man! the confusion of my mind began to subside into thought; I had time to weep!

I turned with the last farewell upon my lips, when I observed old Edwards standing behind me. I looked him full in the face; but his eye was fixed on another object: he pressed between me and the bed, and stood gazing on the breathless remains of his benefactor. I spoke to him I know not what; but he took no notice of what I said, and remained in the same attitude as before. He stood some minutes in that posture, then turned and walked towards the door. He paused as he went;—he returned a second time: I could observe his lips move as he looked: but the voice they would have uttered was lost. He attempted going again; and a third time he returned as before.—I saw him wipe his cheek: then covering his face with his hands, his breast heaving with the most convulsive throbs, he flung out of the room.

———

THE CONCLUSION

HE had hinted that he should like to be buried in a certain spot near the grave of his mother. This is a weakness; but it is universally incident to humanity: 'tis at least a memorial for those who survive: for some indeed a slender memorial will serve; and the soft affections, when they are busy that way, will build their structures, were it but on the paring of a nail.

He was buried in the place he had desired. It was shaded by an old tree, the only one in the church-yard, in which was a cavity worn by time. I have sat with him in it, and counted the tombs. The last time we passed there, methought he looked wistfully on the tree: there was a branch of it that bent towards us waving in the wind; he waved his hand as if he mimicked its motion. There was something predictive in his look! perhaps it is foolish to remark it; but there are times and places when I am a child at those things.

I sometimes visit his grave; I sit in the hollow of the tree.

THE MAN OF FEELING

It is worth a thousand homilies; every noble feeling rises within me! every beat of my heart awakens a virtue!—but it will make you hate the world——No: there is such an air of gentleness around, that I can hate nothing; but, as to the world—I pity the men of it.